D0994930

YOUR ARTERIES CAN CLEAN THEMSELVES

By
Alexis Amziev

ISBN 1-85779-763-9

YOUR ARTERIES CAN CLEAN THEMSELVES
Alexis Amziev

First published in Great Britain MCMXCV by Carnell plc.
28 Eccleston Square, London SW1V 1PU.

© Copyright Idégraf 1995.

This edition copyright © MCMXCV by Carnell plc.

Typeset by Typesetting Solutions, Slough, Berks.
Printed by Repro City Limited, London.

ISBN 1-85779-763-9

All rights reserved. No part of this book may be transmitted, quoted (orally or written), reproduced by any means whatsoever, whether electronic or mechanical, which includes photocopying, photographing, aural or written recording, or stored in any form of retrieval apparatus without the written consent and permission of the author and the publisher.

This book is designed, as far as possible, to meet everyone's needs. Those who mainly wish to be given practical advice can start with the Preface and then move on directly to Chapter 6. Those interested in more scientific explanations will be interested in reading Chapters 1 to 5 and the Annexes.

Contents

CONTENTS

Preface

Of all the illnesses directly linked to living conditions in the developed countries, disorders of the cardiovascular system are the most widespread and above all the most feared: they represent, in fact, the main cause of death in adults.

The scientific and medical world has made major discoveries and yet it seems that nothing will stop the disturbing development of cardiovascular illnesses!

From the evidence, we therefore need to ask ourselves, not about the abilities and competence of the medical profession, but about individuals' ways of life.

The fundamental cause of cardiovascular illnesses, with a few rare exceptions, stems from the unsuitability of lifestyle, and in particular of diet, in relation to the vital, natural needs of the body.

Modern man no longer takes account of the demands of his body to maintain it in good shape. He pressurises it and stresses it a little more every day and eventually wears it out prematurely, deforms it and prevents it from functioning properly.

The body is a complex machine designed by nature to adapt to environmental changes. But by subjecting the body to extreme conditions we finally exhaust all the resources of its self-regulating mechanisms. This is where the real cause of the illnesses which accompany 'civilisation' lies: cardiovascular disorders and most especially arterial complaints, and most degenerative illnesses.

However, those modern scourges are not in any way inevitable. Apart from congenital malformations, *'the majority of cardiac disorders',* stresses the famous South African heart surgeon Christian Barnard, *'are not the same as these disasters against which we can do nothing but rather they are the result of a certain lifestyle. We ourselves create our own illnesses. Heart disease, by far the most widespread and devastating is coronary disease. Without doubt it is the scourge of our modern societies, who are rich and too well-fed'.*

It has been possible to confirm scientifically, in regions of the world where living conditions and, in particular, the natural diet, have scarcely changed for centuries, that cardiovascular diseases have remained very low, practically non-existent. The cause and effect relationship between denatured food and cardiovascular disorders is, therefore, quite clear. Our arteries, in particular, become blocked because of bad eating habits.

It is, therefore, possible to avert these terrible disorders, to improve our condition, even cure it when the illness has not reached a serious, advanced stage. How? First by having some knowledge of the mechanisms of these illnesses. Then, and especially, by adopting a different way of life and eating: dozens of medical and scientific studies conducted throughout the world, in particular in the more developed countries, have demonstrated this beyond question.

The reader must firmly grasp this simple truth: it is up to him alone to protect and if possible cure himself of the cardiovascular scourge. Your arteries can clean themselves, if you eat the right food. This book will help you to do this.

Chapter 1

The arteries and their role

The arteries are blood vessels, forming a huge, branching network which carries blood pumped out from the heart to the different parts and tissues of the body. The arterial system has its counterpart in the venous system, a vascular network which carries blood back to the heart.

In principle, the arteries carry oxygenated blood, whereas the veins carry back blood which has been deprived of oxygen so that it can be reoxygenated.

Two exceptions should be noted: in the minor circulation the pulmonary artery carries non-oxygenated blood from the right ventricle to the lungs, whence it is carried back, after reoxygenation, to the left ventricle of the heart by the pulmonary vein.

The arterial network consists of vessels whose size (diameter) decreases the further away from the heart they are.

The biggest and most important artery is the aorta, which starts on the left ventricle from which it is separated by the aortic sigmoid valves. It forms a curve (aortic arch), then runs down the length of the vertebral column; after crossing the diaphragm it enters the abdomen, where it subdivides into two symmetrical branches, the primitive iliac arteries, close to the entry to the small pelvis.

These two branches in turn subdivide, giving rise, in particular, to the femoral arteries, which branch out, and so on, up to the arterioles and the capillaries. Collateral, rising branches start from the aorta to irrigate the trunk, the upper limbs and the head.

The coronary arteries, which have the vital role of irrigating the cardiac muscle and are crucially important in what is commonly known as a 'heart attack', start just after the sigmoid valves.

A number of arterial stems start from the aortic arch: the brachycephalic, where the right, primitive carotid and the right subclavian originate and whose ramifications provide irrigation of the front part of the head and brain and also of the right upper limb; a symmetrical trunk gives rise, a little higher, to the left primitive carotid and the left subclavian (similar to those on the right-hand side); the vertebral artery, which provides vascularisation of the rear part of the brain (basilar trunk), starts from the left subclavian. The brain is, therefore, irrigated at the rear by the vertebro-basilar system and at the front by the carotid system.

The structure of the arteries varies according to the calibre of the vessels. The largest of these, such as the aorta or the carotids, for example, appear as pipes formed by three layers of different tissue superimposed concentrically: these are the arterial membranes.

The deepest of these, which because of this is called the intima, consists of tissue, having no roughness, the vascular endothelium, formed by smooth, muscular cells and collagenous fibres: this membrane, which is perfectly smooth in its normal state, is in direct contact with the blood flow which it allows to circulate without any turbulence.

The second membrane, between the intima and the covering membrane, is called the media. It consists mainly of muscular fibres which enable it to play a dual role: maintaining the artery at a certain calibre even when it is empty, and therefore giving it a certain rigidity and, in particular, enabling the diameter of the vessel to vary by expanding or contracting.

This last mechanism, vasodilation and vasoconstriction, is regulated by nerve fibres, distributed along the full length of the artery and which are part of the neurovegetative system (and are, therefore, independent of the will of the subject, hence the importance of psychosomatic factors in certain arterial diseases).

Finally, the third membrane, the most superficial, known as the adventitious, acts as a covering and support tissue for the vessel. Consisting of a tissue comparable to the connective tissue of the remaining organs, it makes it possible to attach the artery to the neighbouring anatomical structures. It should be noted that the biggest arteries also have a fine network of blood vessels, the vasa vasorum, which provides vascularisation.

The small arteries, arterioles and capillaries have much less elaborate and solid structures. Indeed, the closer the arteries are to the heart, the more the blood flow is under high pressure (140mm of mercury in the aorta): in order to withstand these pressures they must be of proportional strength and elasticity.

Conversely, pressure falls the further removed it is from the heart; it is not, therefore, necessary for the walls of the farthest-removed vessels to be robust enough to withstand any test.

The essential role of the arterial system is to distribute blood which is rich in oxygen and vital nutritive elements throughout the body. Any cells and tissues which no longer receive these supplies die (necrosis).

It is clear that the disorders which can affect this system often lead to dramatic and even catastrophic situations.

Chapter 2

Disorders of the arteries

Pathology of the arteries is, unfortunately, abundant and varied. There are three main forms of illness: congenital disorders (malformations and others), disorders of an inflammatory nature referred to under the generic name arteritis, and finally chronic illnesses of a degenerative type grouped under the name arteriosclerosis.

The latter are, by far, the most frequent (95 per cent of all arterial pathology) and the most deadly (over 50 per cent of deaths from all causes taken together in developed societies, or twice as deadly as cancer).

Arteriosclerosis is defined as a hardening, a thickening of the arteries, with or without deposits on the arterial walls, culminating in an impairment of these vessels (atrophy, calcification, etc.) and to serious blood circulation disorders.

Atherosclerosis is the most widespread form of arteriosclerosis and the most dangerous: this is the one which particularly interests us, as it corresponds to the 'civilisation illness' definition, in the sense that it is closely connected to lifestyle and can be prevented and even cured by reorganising the way we live, in particular as regards eating habits.

What is atherosclerosis?

As its name indicates, atherosclerosis is arteriosclerosis caused by atheroma, that is, an excess amount of fat on the artery walls, especially the two coronary arteries which become hard and thick, lose their elasticity and are lined with a deposit of lipidic and calcareous substances. Finally, the lesions can cause obstructions or ruptures of the injured vessels.

The formation of atheromas does not take place overnight and atherosclerosis appears in a number of different ways depending on the seat of the lesions and how serious they are.

The most frequent localisation is, of course, the cardiac region (20 per cent of deaths) and affects five times as many men as women, but also the cerebral region (15 per cent of deaths). There again, there are four men to one woman among the victims. Another fairly frequent localisation is atherosclerosis of the lower limbs, which translates into severe arteritis of these limbs. (You will find more details in Annexe A).

Can the risks be limited?

Epidemiological studies of atherosclerosis have not yet made it possible to draw up a very precise aetiology of the illness. However, researchers have recorded a certain number of what are known as risk factors, as there is no single, universal cause for the ailment. Nor have these risk factors an equal 'epidemiological weight': some appear to be more atherogenous (capable of stimulating the production of atheromas) than others. However, even more important, it is the coexistence of at least two factors which are more or less atherogenous in the same individual which makes it possible to produce fairly reliable prognoses.

The risk factor which is best known to the general public is cholesterol, or more precisely an excess of it in the body. So many things have been said and written about it, from the most serious to the most irrational, that we have decided to devote a special chapter to it (see Chapter 3) to make the point objectively, taking account of the latest medical knowledge.

These risk factors cannot be changed

Heredity. – Statistically, it has been established that there are family backgrounds which are more favourable than others to the appearance of atherosclerosis. Thus an individual who had a brother or sister who died from ischaemic cardiopathy before the age of 60 sees his risk of death from heart disease doubled. However, the interpretation of this statistical fact is extremely difficult: what is the part played by a possible congenital weakness in the arterial wall? What does the part play which pertains to a shared family lifestyle (food, lack of exercise, etc.)? What is the part which can be related to family predisposition to certain disorders, such as diabetes or hyperlipidaemia? It is impossible to answer these questions, or many others, precisely, given our present state of knowledge.

Sex. – All medical research is in agreement in recognising a much stronger predisposition to atherosclerosis in men than in women. With the latter the disorder appears, on average, ten to fifteen years later than in men (except in certain circumstances, in the event of an ovariectomy, for example). It would appear that the secretion of oestrogen by the ovaries plays an important role in protecting the arterial walls.

Age. – Except for a number of rare cases of congenital abnormalities, atherosclerosis appears belatedly (after 45 in men, 55 in women). This is explained, on the one hand, by the natural ageing of the body (the regulation and defence mechanisms are more effective in the young) and, on the other, by the fact that atherosclerosis is a chronic illness which takes several years to appear clinically.

The menopause. – Age for age, women who have been through the menopause have a higher atherosclerosis risk than women who have not yet started the menopause. This can be explained by the ceasing of oestrogen secretions whose protective role on the arterial walls has been highlighted. Certain specialists, such as Dr Apfelbaum, recommend preventative oestrogen therapy for all women who have been through the menopause, and also for young women who have undergone surgical ablation of the ovaries (unless there is a contraindication, particularly ovariectomy during the treatment of breast cancer.

These risk factors can be changed

High blood pressure. – This is a sure coronary risk factor and an even greater cerebral vascular risk. It severely aggravates the ischaemic cardiopathies: an atherosclerotic person suffering from hypertension has a four times greater risk of dying from a complication of the illness than a person with atherosclerosis who is not suffering from hypertension. Moreover, high blood pressure is directly responsible for lesions of the arterial wall, in particular by impairing elasticity, which contributes to the appearance and installation of atheromas. We should remember that blood pressure values must normally be lower than 140mm Hg for systolic pressure and 90mm Hg for diastolic pressure.

Tobacco dependency. – This is one of the essential factors of cardiovascular illnesses. Epidemiological investigations have shown that, towards their fifties, heavy smokers have cardiovascular mortality three times higher than that of non-smokers. The risk is proportional to the period of dependency (the younger the age when starting smoking, the greater the risk is increased), to the number of cigarettes smoked daily (smoking twenty cigarettes a day doubles the risk of a heart attack; smoking fifty cigarettes, the risk is multiplied by ten) and to the type of tobacco dependency (inhaling cigarette smoke is an aggravating factor; pipes and cigars are relatively less harmful). An inquiry conducted by the British Heart Foundation showed that if the population of Britain were to stop smoking, between ten and fifteen thousand lives would be saved each year.

The harmfulness of cigarette smoke is due to certain of its constituents, the most dangerous of which are carbon monoxide and nicotine. Carbon monoxide (CO), which is also produced by a number of sources in modern life, such as cars, is caused by the combustion of tobacco and the paper in which it is wrapped. CO acts directly on the composition of the blood in two ways. On the one hand, by combining with haemoglobin in the red corpuscles, it significantly reduces their ability to carry oxygen, hence poor blood oxygenation. On the other, and this is the most dangerous aspect, the CO acts on the composition of the platelets.

The process, which has been brought to light by researchers, is as follows: platelets are formed in the lung vessels by the division of larger structures carried by the blood at the time when it is oxygenated. However, the division of these structures is seriously disrupted by the presence of cigarette smoke and therefore of CO in the lungs: instead of having platelets of a normal size in the oxygenated blood which travels back to the heart in order to be distributed by the arterial network, we find larger-sized platelets which also show abnormal viscosity. The blood becomes more easily coagulable and the risks of thrombosis considerably higher: the presence of an atheromatous plaque in an artery further aggravates the situation, as even normal platelets have a tendency to adhere to it.

Painstaking studies have shown beyond any doubt what the reality of this process is: analysis of the blood of individuals with heart disease and of the blood of healthy individuals has clearly shown the presence of large, high-viscosity platelets in the former and normal platelets in the latter.

The nicotine in tobacco, for its part, plays a disastrous role. This stimulant activates the pathogenic secretion of adrenalin. However, adrenalin, a hormone normally secreted by the suprarenal gland, has a number of important actions: it accelerates the heart beat rate, increases the strength and amplitude of heartbeats, contracts the peripheral vessels (vasoconstriction), but dilates the coronary arteries (vasodilation), raises blood pressure and glycaemia and inhibits the bronchial muscle structure.

In its normal physiological state the body secretes another hormone, acetylcholine, which opposes the action of the adrenalin, so that it establishes a perfect balance between the two antagonistic hormones. The introduction of a stimulant for the secretion of adrenalin, nicotine, therefore breaks this natural balance: thus the effects of the adrenalin are not counterbalanced by those of the acetylcholine and therefore become potentially pathogenic. The havoc wreaked by this situation in the long-term can well be imagined ...

To summarise, therefore, tobacco dependency is shown to be a powerful atherogenous factor through the combination of the disastrous effects of nicotine, carbon monoxide and smoke and other constituents. Alone, it represents 35 per cent of the coronary risk!

Obesity. – This is another major risk factor for atherosclerosis. Scientific data is available to prove this fully. Here are a few examples:

- a study performed on 1,000 autopsies on individuals aged over 35 by Wilens, an American, showed two and a half times as many cases of arteriosclerosis in obese men as in those of normal weight;

- another study covering over 5,000 individuals and prepared over eighteen years proved a strong incidence of obesity on coronary troubles, myocardial infarction, brain haemorrhages and left cardiac failures;

- finally, another investigation covering 80 young American soldiers who died of an infarction or coronaritis showed that 73 of them were typical obese persons.

For their part, Drs Creff and Herschberg stress quite plainly that 'whatever the case, the clinical fact is indisputable: excess weight is accompanied by a high incidence of arteriosclerotic illnesses in obese androids. Angina pectoris appears among them both much more often and above all earlier'.

Indeed, obesity, which is always a disorder of eating habits, is associated with the other risk factors which it creates: high blood pressure, diabetes, hypercholesterolaemia and hypertriglycidaemia. In addition, from the anatomical point of view, the heart in obese people is surrounded by a fatty layer which becomes thicker along the intercavitary fissures and the coronary arteries and displays fatty infiltration of the myocardium.

Some other risk factors

Diabetes is not specifically a risk factor in heart disease. However, its most fearsome complications, since we have learned how to control the terrible acidocetosic comas, are atherosclerosis, arteriopathies of the lower limbs and cerebral vascular troubles.

Gout, or hyperuricaemia, is not a specific risk factor either. However, as it is often associated with a number of atherogenous illnesses or complaints (high blood pressure, obesity, diabetes, etc.) diagnosis of it in an individual who is also predisposed to atherosclerosis is not a small risk element.

Certain oral contraceptives produce aggravation of cardiovascular risk after 35, when they are administered to individuals having one or more risk factors (high blood pressure, hypercholesterolaemia and obesity, especially).

Excessive intake of salt in food is an aggravating factor, minimal it is true, but likely to increase blood pressure and therefore atherogenesis.

Alcohol has two facets: taken in moderation it would appear to encourage the 'good' proportion of HDL cholesterol (see p. 120). On the other hand, excessive alcohol consumption, whatever form this may take, undoubtedly increases the risk of arteriosclerosis.

Sedentary habits increase overall cardiovascular mortality for both sexes in lesser proportions. Indeed, the absence of physical exercise and poor oxygenation scarcely favour the normal elimination by the body of waste materials and toxins, which have an indisputable atherogenous influence.

In a report in the *Journal of the American College of Cardiology* in August, 1993, it was confirmed that among people who have exercised intensively for between five and six hours a week for just one year, a regression of atherosclerosis was recorded. The report indicates that the change in lifestyle, without medicines or surgery, can halt and even partially reverse the cholesterol and fatty deposits build-up process on the arterial walls.

Naturally, intensive exercise, (jogging, power walking, competitive swimming, etc.) must be approved by your doctor according to the condition of your heart.

The individual's psychological profile can also be a risk factor. People predisposed or subjected to stress, who are overambitious and forced to lead a 'life of hell' (inflexible hours, permanent pressure in their professional circle . . .) have an aggravated risk of heart disease, independently of the other risk factors. We should be aware, for example, that stress has significant hormonal repercussions: in particular it triggers off a hypersecretion of adrenalin. However, we have seen, in connection with tobacco dependency, the atherogenous harm caused by this hormone when secretion of it is not correctly balanced by an adequate secretion of its antagonistic hormone, acetylcholine.

To summarise:

1. Arteriosclerosis and atherosclerosis, which are chronic degenerative disorders, do not have one single cause in the same way that it can be stated that the Koch bacillus is responsible for pulmonary tuberculosis.

2. These disorders are caused, after years of silent evolution, by very varied factors.

3. Each of these risk factors has quite a serious incidence on the evolution of the illness towards a dangerous stage.

4. It is the combination of two or more risk factors which leads to the dramatic outcome of infarction or a cerebral attack; the more an individual has simultaneous risk factors, the more dangerous his position becomes; men of over 45 are in greater danger than women of the same age; the woman who has passed through the menopause is more vulnerable than a woman of the same age who has not.

5. The role of cholesterol is much-debated: is it directly responsible for atheromatous disorder, as some people maintain? Or is its presence in atheromas merely the result of a complex pathological process, as others maintain? This is what we shall try to make clear in the next chapter.

Chapter 3

How you can combat cholesterol

The greater part of the medical profession accepts a relationship between excess blood cholesterol and athero-sclerosis, especially with a coronary localisation. However, when we examine this more closely, matters are far from being simple and obvious. That is due to the nature of 'cholesterol' itself and the complexity of the biological phenomena concerned.

What is cholesterol?

It is a kind of sterol, a secondary complex alcohol in solid form (crystals), with a polycyclic nucleus, and is found in a number of organic tissues and body-fluids: cell membranes, particularly those in the brain, sex hormones, cortico-steroids, bile acids, etc. It is a biological element of major importance and is absolutely indispensable to life.

Cholesterol belongs to the lipids group: it is soluble in fats, but not in water. Circulation of it in the body is rigorously controlled (see Annexe B).

The body is, moreover, incapable of destroying the tiniest molecule of cholesterol. It must either continuously recycle it or evacuate it in part with the faeces. This fact is not the least important in the process.

The cholesterol requirements of a healthy adult are in the order of one gramme and a half per day. The supply comes from two sources: the endogenous source corresponds to the synthesis of cholesterol by the liver and supplies two thirds of requirements; the exogenous source is made up by the supply of cholesterol present in a certain number of foods and supplies the other third. The amount of cholesterol depends, therefore, on a number of factors, but mainly on the hepatic function and the nature of the food consumed daily by each individual.

A lot has been said and written about cholesterol and much of it is inconsistent.

For years the effectiveness of anticholesterol diets has been proclaimed, in particular eliminating a certain number of fatty products such as butter and animal fats, and all kinds of low-fat products are manufactured, implying that they help to lower the cholesterol level.

How should we see all that?

First of all, let us make a comparison between different countries.

In France, where a great deal of butter and animal fats are consumed, the rate of heart complaints, even though it has multiplied by 35 since the start of the century, is much lower than in the United States where, for thirty years now, the war against cholesterol and fats of animal origin has been waged on all fronts.

Perhaps you will say that heart complaints and the cholesterol level are two different things. Quite so. It has by no means been proved that a high cholesterol level increases the risk of heart complaints. We do not intend here to attack the pharmaceutical laboratories or the food industry which, each in their own field, are making considerable progress which benefits public health.

However, in this matter of cholesterol, we still have the impression that the laboratories are doing well out of this anticholesterol war, thanks to their many special lines for lowering cholesterol levels.

The food industry, for its part, also does well out of the fashion for reduced-fat products and a great number of articles in the press, perhaps not entirely disinterested, have helped to encourage the consumption of manufactured products replacing butter or fat-reduced products and, also of a certain number of foods whose composition allows people to think that they will help the fight against cholesterol.

Medical publications offer controversial opinions on this subject. This is how the *New England Journal of Medicine*, which is well-known to doctors throughout the world, adopted the anticholesterol attitude 100 per cent. In this journal we read that 'the ideal cholesterol intake is probably zero, which means that we need to avoid any product of animal origin'. We shall see later that other medical journals do not fully share this point of view and sometimes even oppose it.

If we now resume comparisons with other countries, we see that certain peoples in Africa, such as the Samburu, who obviously are unaware of anything involving cholesterol problems and eat as much animal fat as they can, do not in any way appear to be predisposed to heart complaints, any more than to an excess of cholesterol, or the blocking of their arteries.

Let us continue our tour around Africa.

The Samburu tribe, which lives in the North of Kenya, consumes between 300 and 400g of fats of animal origin each day, supplying a normal level of cholesterol. However, they are not the only people in Africa who consume animal fats.

The Karimojong, in Uganda, live solely on products of animal origin, milk, meat and their cattle. They are rarely subject to heart complaints.

Still in Africa the Masai, in Southern Kenya, have a diet consisting of 60 per cent products of animal origin and animal fats. Their cholesterol level, nevertheless, is normal.

The normal cholesterol level for an American over 55 is 234, the average level for an African is 122. There is a temptation to explain these differences by genetics. But it has been established that black people who leave Africa and live in Europe or the United States and consume the same types of food as their country of adoption see their cholesterol levels and heart complaints rates rise to the same levels as those of the host nation. It would, therefore, certainly appear that in addition to living conditions, food plays a leading part in this field.

In the Indies, as in Africa, people eat a lot of products of animal origin and absolutely no increase in the cholesterol level of the people there has been recorded.

Dr Serge Renaud explained on television that the Mediterranean people (such as the Cretans) who eat olive oil and purslane are less affected than others by heart complaints and do not have a particularly low cholesterol level. Olive oil and purslane appear to play a protective role against the risks produced by other foods. It is, therefore, clear that diet plays a vital part in the development of atheromatous deposits and heart complaints.

Dr Michel de Lorgeril, who works with Dr Renaud, states that *'looking back, it can now be said that a number of major mistakes have been made. It had been noticed that cardio-vascular mortality rates were increasing with the supply of foods containing saturated fats. Some people then thought that they could state that this mortality was also increasing with blood cholesterol levels and, finally, that these levels were correlated to the food supply containing fats. This was at the root of a great number of mistakes and a great number of untruths. Contrary to what is regularly stated, none of the studies in which it has been sought to reduce blood cholesterol levels have made it possible to improve the survival rate, and all pharmacological or nutritional interventions seeking to reduce mortality by lowering cholesterol levels have failed'* (*Le Monde*, 11th June, 1994).

It is not our intention to cut short this debate which divides medicine but which, at the present time, favours those who are in favour of a fight against cholesterol. This is, moreover, quite normal, because in the absence of certainties a doctor prefers to advise you to keep off fatty products of animal origin rather than leave you in ignorance and make you run an additional risk. He will adopt and maintain this attitude until clearer proofs are established.

On the other hand, what is not yet known is whether attempts to lower the cholesterol level in an individual cause other problems. Changes in the cholesterol level are, perhaps, part of a self-protecting mechanism for the body and attempts to lower this level may be harmful. We would repeat that nothing is certain yet in this field.

(In Annexe C you will find the different medicines currently used in the treatment of hypercholesterolaemia but we wish to stress this point once more: you should never resort to hypolipidaemiant medicines without specific instructions from your doctor, and then only having tried unsuccessfully to correct the problem through an appropriate diet under the supervision of the doctor. This precept holds good for all types of hyperlipidaemia except for hypercholesterolaemia in families, where the doctor can instantly commence medicinal treatment.)

It would appear, for example, that for many of us the intake of foods which are very high in cholesterol increases our own cholesterol level only very temporarily, with the body producing normal self-regulation.

Dr Macnamara, of Rockefeller University in the United States, performed an experiment by giving 50 people a diet containing a considerable amount of food with a high cholesterol content. He established, by painstaking tests, that most patients absorbed less cholesterol through their intestines in spite of the superabundance of this substance in their food.

Dr Macnamara also performed observations comparing a group of people subsisting as much as possible on foods which were exceptionally rich in cholesterol and a group which subsisted only on white meats such as rabbit, meat which is low in fat such as horse, vegetable oils and all other products with a low cholesterol content. He noted that the difference in cholesterol levels between the two groups was only 8 per cent. However, with individuals there may, from day to day, be differences of between 15 and 20 per cent in the cholesterol level. The question arises, therefore, whether the medicines intended to lower the cholesterol level are really necessary and whether or not they do as much harm as they do good.

It has also been noted that among all the people with heart complaints only 10 per cent have an extremely high cholesterol level. Conversely, many of them suffer from this devastating illness while at the same time having a normal cholesterol level.

It has further been noted that often, after the heart complaint, the cholesterol level increases. This further adds to the confusion on the subject.

Let us come now to the problems of deposits on the arteries, which particularly interest us in this book.

Dr P. Bendett, of the University of Washington, demonstrated that arterial deposits contained very little cholesterol. These arterial deposits consist of cells which have migrated from the intermediate layer of the arterial membrane to the inside. It is not, therefore, cholesterol which produces these arterial deposits.

We believe that all the traditional anticholesterol diets which forbid you to have food with a high cholesterol content in your diet, have not yet been justified by experience and this phrase is a euphemism.

The diet which we recommend in this book and which you are about to discover, seeks to provide more room for fresh, natural foods and eliminate all foods which have been processed. It is difficult to accept that a completely artificial product, such as margarine, can be better for the body than a natural product like butter.

Why should you deprive yourself of a healthy food, provided that you eat a reasonable amount of it, and eat products whose composition and processing are completely unknown to you?

Cholesterol treatments

Medicinal treatments should, by their very nature, be reserved for severe cases of hypercholesterolaemia. For the treatment of the least serious hypercholesterolaemia a dietetic regimen, if perfectly adapted to each individual, can produce positive effects – at least if we consider that the goal to be achieved is essentially that of reducing the total cholesterol level to normal or close to normal. Nevertheless, a dietetic regimen, however 'well-targeted' it may be, is not a panacea.

Indeed, all diets, and especially those referred to as hypocholesterolemiant, have drawbacks, sometimes dangers; these are unquestionable and numerous:

- It is possible, in fact, to achieve a significant fall in total cholesterol (ChT) by means of an appropriate dietetic regimen. However, this fall will affect LDL cholesterol just as much as HDL, which is normal.

    (This is where the position may become dangerous. If, before the diet, a person has fairly high total cholesterol (between 2.5 and 3) and a good HDL level equal to, or higher than, 0.70, after a few weeks or months on the diet it is possible to 'go back down' to a ChT level below 2.5 (which is good), but with an HDL level equal to, or lower than, 0.40. We are aware, however, of the crucial importance of the HDL level and the LDL/HDL ratio (see p. 120). It is noted here, therefore, that the patient will be in a much more serious coronary risk situation and this after weeks or months of all kinds of hardships and restrictions! The problem is extremely complex, as it is very difficult to establish a dietetic regimen which preserves the HDL while at the same time reducing the LDL.)

- Any diet involving strict food bans can, over a period, result in certain mineral or vitamin deficiencies. These are difficult to correct, as they become established progressively and insidiously; what is more, they are often revealed by their clinical manifestations, that is, when the damage has already been done.

- The favourable effects of diets are never obtained conclusively. People who follow slimming diets know this very well: as soon as the restrictions are lifted they unfailingly put back the pounds so painfully lost and sometimes even more. This also applies to anticholesterol diets: the ChT level rises inexorably again as soon as the dietetic instructions are no longer being followed.

- The negative psychological effects of diets should not be neglected: months, if not years, of discipline, limitations and restrictions finally cause stress, neurasthenia, even neuroses – with all their social, family and professional consequences . . .

- A diet which has been successfully tried by a friend or relative should not be followed, nor should a diet which one improvises oneself after having read articles in magazines about foods or groups of foods accused of all coronary troubles. The same dietetic regimen may prove positive for one person and harmful for another. So beware!

In conclusion, we should bear in mind:

1. When the total cholesterol level is high (above 3g/l) it is vital to consult a doctor, even with a very good HDL

level (higher than 0.70). The use of hypolipaemiants must be resorted to only on express instructions from the doctor.

2. When the total cholesterol level is moderately high (between 2.5 and 3g/l) with a good HDL level (between 0.50 and 0.70 or over), a moderate hypocholesterolaemiant diet under medical supervision is sufficient to re-establish normality, without the need for any medicines.

3. Concurrently with the treatment, the other coronary risk factors, if any, must be eliminated (tobacco dependency, obesity, etc.).

However, a return to a normal cholesterolaemic situation does not eliminate the danger of a relapse, nor the morbid evolution of atheromas which may already be established. In order to avoid these risks, or in any case to limit vulnerability to them, there is a natural, simple method which can be used, absolutely without any detriment, even indirect, this is the Fresh Food Method.

Recommended some twenty years ago by Robert S. Ford, in his book *Foods which Cure*, this method is a course of treatment, both preventative and curative, against the danger of arteriosclerosis and atherosclerosis. Thanks to this work and other internationally-famous dieticians, we give you a complete, practical nutrition programme based on fresh food, which will give you the best possible arterial protection and help your arteries to clear themselves, progressively, of the deposits clogging them.

Chapter 4

Better arteries, thanks to fresh food

Just like any living organism, the human body constantly needs to be provided with remarkably varied substances in order to continue to remain alive, grow, maintain itself and repair itself as the need arises. This is what is meant by nutrition. It includes the oxygen in the air we breath, water and a number of foods of animal and vegetable origin which we ingest.

Indeed, contrary to what we may be tempted to think *a priori,* the adult body is not fashioned once and for all when fully grown, following on childhood and adolescence.

Our body cells are also being continually renewed, they grow, live and die after quite a long time, depending on the variety (and there is a large number of these) of cells. Without supplies of essential nutrients needed to manufacture new cells to replace those which have died, the body would not survive for long.

The human body can be compared with an ultra-sophisticated machine capable of 'processing' nutritional elements: it uses them for producing energy and various substances and creating new biological entities, such as hormones or enzymes, for example.

More precisely, it has a number of highly complex self-cleaning systems which enable it to reject and eliminate the waste produced by this transformation work, unused materials and waste generated by its own functions.

Thus it rids itself of carbon dioxide by the respiration mechanism; it evacuates non-assimilable or useless food through the faecal bolus; it expels dead cells and micro-organisms (a process which is particularly evident in the case of an abscess).

Indeed, it has sophisticated mechanisms which ensure the expulsion of any undesirable foreign bodies (the most simple example being the profuse secretion of tears when you have something in your eye). Each organ has its own independent self-cleaning system. The kidneys would very quickly become blocked by phosphates and other mineral waste if they did not have a self-cleaning system.

Likewise the liver, that incredible factory which functions without stopping, would quickly become clogged by waste from the various metabolisms with which it is concerned, without its permanent self-drainage arrangement.

The same applies to the blood vessels, particularly the arteries: they are equipped with a self-cleaning mechanism which eliminates the particles which inconveniently adhere to their walls.

The tuning of this remarkable machine by nature is not carried out overnight. Millions of years of trial and error, changes and evolution must have been needed before achieving the result which we are describing. However, the 'model' on which the final product was produced was pre-historic man, a creature whose food was very close to nature:

'All foods come from plants and animals', remarks Robert S. Ford, *'on which the human race has lived directly for hundreds of thousands of years, when man was simply a food gatherer and animal hunter, when he ate tender leaves, nuts, roots, fruits and the flesh of the fish and mammals which he was able to capture, most of the time raw and fresh. This is the type of food for which Nature designed the human body'.*

Morphological study of prehistoric man shows us that he had a stronger skeleton than that of our contemporaries in the developed countries and in many others which are less rich but have adopted Western eating habits, proving that his diet endowed him with a remarkable constitution.

Studying the nutrition and health of isolated peoples who have remained close to the prehistoric way of life provides us with additional evidence regarding the benefits of a natural, fresh diet. A number of scientists have shown that neither the Bantu, nor the Pygmies of Central Africa, nor the Papuans of New Guinea, who have remained faithful to their ancestral eating habits, show any of the degenerative illnesses which are rampant on a vast scale in the industrialised countries.

More striking is the observation made some years ago by Dr Weston Price ... in Switzerland, a highly developed, civilised country: *'In the high valleys of this country, all environmental factors are strictly identical, from one group to another, except for food.*

'Thus in Vissoie and Ayer, two villages which are separated by a few hours' walk, clothes, houses, farms, cultures and customs are exactly the same. But whereas in Ayer, an isolated village, the inhabitants eat local products on the spot, in Vissoie, which is linked to the outside world by a road, the country people sell their high quality rye and dairy produce and eat modern food. The

signs of degeneracy appear immediately.'

Another example is provided by the Japanese. Japan is one of the countries in which cardiovascular illnesses are least frequent (four times less than in the United States).

The traditional food consists mainly of fresh food, usually eaten raw (especially fish). However, Japanese who have emigrated and settled in the United States and who have adopted the American eating model, have exactly the same frequency of cardiovascular illnesses as their new fellow countrymen.

More striking still is the observation performed in the leisured social classes in Japan itself: this section of the population, which has followed the American nutritional model to the detriment of the indigenous model, has a mortality rate caused by cardiovascular illnesses which is identical to that of the United States.

This, then, is clear evidence that there is a very close cause and effect relationship between eating habits and degenerative illnesses, as the comparison between two population groups of the same origin, having an identical culture, differing only by their diet, shows, throughout the world, a correlation between industrial type food and degenerative illnesses, and a correlation between traditional type food and the absence of these illnesses.

It remains to ask why . . . ?

We have already emphasised the importance of the cholesterol factor in arteriosclerotic processes and we shall come back to this a little further on.

However, food in the developed countries is not characterised only by its excessive richness in fats, in particular animal fats: foods of all kinds also have harmful properties which largely contribute to triggering off degenerative disorders.

These foods are subjected to serious damage before even reaching the consumer; the consumer, who is badly-informed, exacerbates this situation by his lack of knowledge as regards the choice, preparation, storage and ingestion of food. Let us examine each of these points carefully.

a) Denatured farm produce

The basis of all human food is plants. This applies to fruit and vegetables. However, it also applies to meat, milk and dairy products and even fish: these products are plants converted by animals, whether large or small. Our health depends, therefore, to a large extent on agricultural production methods. Do present industrial methods meet the nutritional requirements of food for human beings?

Let us state, quite plainly, that it is not our intention to cry over an irretrievably lost past, nor to try to go back to the days of sailing ships and paraffin lamps. It is a matter of setting out the position, today's realities, as clearly as possible, in order to act with full knowledge of the facts, and avoid making mistakes which could have serious consequences.

Until the last century, in Europe, farming methods had changed very little since ancient times. Plots of land were cultivated and these were then left to rest (fallow), while new plots a little further away were cleared for planting. This system had the twin advantage of allowing cultivation on naturally-fertile soils, without exhausting the old plots which were spread with vital mineral elements in the form of manure, thus making them fertile again after a few seasons. However, the surfaces suitable for cultivation cannot, unfortunately, be extended indefinitely. And so, with the lightning population growth, it soon became necessary to resort to intensive farming methods, which resulted in:

• contributing to the erosion of arable soils, turned over too often and, having been laid bare, directly exposed to rain action, which dissolved the mineral elements and washed them into the streams, rivers and the sea;

• exhausting the land because of the lack of dung and natural fertiliser which alone are able to return the minerals which the crops have taken out of the soil.

In order to remedy this situation, chemical fertilisers were invented and these were used immediately and injudiciously over vast areas. These fertilisers, which are over-rich in nitrogen and potash, did not, however, supply sufficient other minerals such as calcium, iron, sodium, magnesium, etc. And so soils became progressively acid, encouraging the proliferation of parasitic micro-organisms (fungi, bacteria . . .). Over the same period, plants cultivated in this way, and therefore badly fed, became weaker. Their natural enemies, insects and other larvae, made the most of this: they multiplied, ravaging vast areas of cultivated land. A remedy, therefore, had to be found: this was the advent of pesticides and other insecticides. Tons of this chemical material were dumped onto the sickly plants . . . veritable poisons for any living thing, and not only for larvae and insects.

The result of this industrial farming method, where it was practised (and where it is, unfortunately, still practised) in an intensive, disorganised manner, was catastrophic. Crops were obtained which were doubly denatured: products were both deficient in minerals and contaminated by toxic substances. Concurrently, the subterranean fauna was practically wiped out by all these chemical products. Earthworms, however, and other creatures living under the ground, play a decisive part in the fertility of the land. It is thanks to their unseen, unceasing activities that the soil is worked in depth, aerated and able to retain rainwater. Without them the ground compacts and becomes like concrete, preventing the plant roots from spreading out so that they can draw, from deep down, on the nutrients they need to be able to grow.

The consequences of this aggression against nature are not limited to this damage. Indeed, enormous quantities of chemical poisons carried along by run-off water and the wind have encroached on pasture and reached the ground water table. Animals for slaughter have in turn been contaminated: traces, sometimes major ones, of chemical products have been discovered in meat from certain regions; milk itself is not spared. As regards the pollution of the ground water table by nitrates the problem, which has still scarcely been touched upon, will arise with terrible urgency by the beginning of the next century.

Human genius, which has always been shrewd, particularly when it is spurred on by the lure of profits, is turning to other 'solutions'. There is talk of genetic manipulation in order to obtain plant species or varieties which are capable of resisting everything. But will people's health resist them?

New farming methods produce mutation products, tomatoes which look like tomatoes, carrots identical in appearance to real carrots, but without their original nutritional value. Shall we soon have to swallow a pill consisting of a cocktail of mineral salts and vitamins to compensate for the deficiencies in our fruits and vegetables? Will the taste of natural products, which is the spice of life, be just a mysterious memory for our great-grandchildren, gleaned from books and videos?

This apocalyptic scene must, however, be qualified. Certainly the majority of farm produce which can be found in supermarkets is of poor nutritional quality because it has been grown in accordance with industrial production methods. But where farmers act with moderation, caution and intelligence in the use of fertilisers and crop protection agents, the products are of a quite acceptable quality and are not dangerous.

Moreover, some farmers continue to produce in accordance with traditional methods (organic crops, with no chemicals used): their products are of excellent quality and are completely free from any harmful content. It is up to the reader to know how to choose, because quite often the quality/price ratio is loaded in favour of the less denatured products.

The adulteration of food products does not take place only during production. Other processes affect their nature before they reach the retailers' stalls. We can quote, among others (but we shall point out the anomalies to be wary of when we come to each group of food later on):

- damaging the integrity of the food (such as, for example, pasteurising milk and dairy products, refining sugar and certain oils using chemical products, polishing cereals, particularly rice, etc.);

- improperly using certain disinfectants for preserving various food products;

- excessively using chemical, hormonal and antibiotic substances in the production and preservation of meat;

- picking immature fruit and maturing it using artificial methods;

- hydrogenating certain fats;

- inappropriately chilling foods which can damage or rot easily, with the resultant appearance of microscopic fungi;

- using certain materials which are unsuitable for packing and preserving 'active' food products; etc.

b) Mistakes made by the consumer

Not only does the consumer often find only somewhat denatured, even adulterated products on the market, but makes mistakes which may worsen the situation. The first mistake relates to the choice of products. Badly informed, the consumer no longer spends time going round the markets or stores comparing products between one and the other.

However, wandering around the market is very good, relaxing; the sight of all those mouth-watering products revives the desire to eat well, and therefore to be more particular about quality ... Unfortunately, going round the market is now quickly over with, like a tiresome duty. If we add badly-interpreted economic considerations to this – believing that the most expensive products are the best precisely because they are the most expensive, which is almost always wrong! – the consumer thinks that it is right to buy food which appears to be of good quality but which in fact is second-rate, for example: white flour, white sugar, polished rice, bread and pastry made of over-refined white flour, low-quality table oils, butter with preservatives added, fruits and vegetables which are immature, or already over-ripe, unattractive-looking, industrially pre-cooked food, literally packed with chemical products, etc. What can we say about those pre-washed salads sold in plastic packaging, that you have only to empty onto your plate and season with a vinaigrette which has also been prepared industrially! We thus eat a perfectly indigestible food, practically devoid of any useful nourishment but packed with harmful substances. In order to convince yourself, carry out this little experiment: wash a salad normally, then put it into a plastic bag and wait for a few hours. Your salad will not take long to start to wilt; bacteria will develop, as will microscopic fungi appearing as dark red scars. If these signs are not apparent in industrially-prepared salads, this is because they have been treated with bactericides and fungicides which continue to act in the intestines to the detriment of the precious intestinal bacterial flora! These are the nutritional absurdities we have come to. And yet what is simpler than washing a good, fresh, crisp salad yourself and seasoning it with just a squeeze of lemon or, better still, eating it just as it is, without any seasoning at all. This is infinitely tastier and you also keep the vitamins and mineral salts in the succulent leaves intact.

Another mistake, which is tending to become more general, consists of eating the same food right through the year. Indeed, nowadays, for shopkeepers, both large and small, the seasons no longer exist: in the middle of winter they have summer products imported at great expense from the antipodes. Of course, in order to be able to withstand the long journey, they are subjected to all kinds of chemical treatments.

But the worst part is that this monotonous diet seriously damages health. Our bodies have been programmed for thousands of years to be fed on products available according to the seasons. Because of this, nutrimental requirements change throughout the year: we need, for example, an iron, calcium and phosphorus supplement in winter in our climate. Formerly, dried vegetables eaten at this time provided a large part of our needs.

However, nowadays, the consumption of lentils, split peas, haricot beans, etc. has almost disappeared from regular use. In spring, summer, autumn and winter we now eat the same foods: this monotony will lead inescapably to deficiencies which will have particular repercussions on the next generation ... And the body's biological rhythm is seriously upset.

The monotony and uniformity of dietary fashion does not spare any age bracket: children, adults, pregnant women or nursing mothers, older people, all eat the same things. However, different people have very different needs. For example, a child has much greater needs as regards calcium, phosphorus, iron, etc., so that its bones are sound and its body develops consistently. Placing it on the same diet as an adult will stunt and even frustrate its growth. It is not by chance that the medical profession has recorded a sharp increase in osteoporosis cases at ever-younger ages. The statement also holds good, of course, for pregnant women or nursing mothers and older people, whose nutritional requirements again are different from those of children and adults.

Whatever the case may be, dietary monotony scarcely favours the self-cleaning mechanisms in the body, with the latter not receiving the substances it needs to perform these functions.

What is more, the consumer makes other mistakes (cooking and preparation methods, portions, etc.) which further accentuate the harmful effects.

Food which is not fresh and has been industrially treated does not supply the needs of the body: on the contrary, it overwhelms it with chemical substances which are not easily assimilated and are generally harmful. But the worst is yet to come. This type of food contains large amounts of 'hidden' fat and cholesterol. These lipids, when brought into contact with certain chemical agents, react:

'Part of the fatty substances and the cholesterol', writes Robert S. Ford, *'is transformed into a calcareous, non-nutritional product which our bodies are unable to use. When we eat this kind of debased food, a part of the calcareous product attaches itself semi-permanently to our arteries; these denatured fats are much more resistant and durable and call to mind dried paint and soap, and also the hard calcareous cakes which clog grease-absorbing filters in kitchens.'*

These calcareous substances, whose precise chemical nature has not yet been reliably established, and which Ford calls 'fatty waste', are found mainly in finely-ground flour, salted or smoked foods such as slicing sausage, bacon, corned beef, ham, foods preserved over a long period in brine or tins, foods cooked at high temperatures, etc. A large part of this waste is, fortunately, evacuated with the sellae. However, another part enters the body through the intestinal mucus, and then spreads throughout the body. Some waste reaches the joints. However, the joint tissues are sparsely vascularised: the waste is blocked there; accumulation of it will, therefore, contribute to the degeneration process which culminates in arthrosis.

Fatty waste has a particular tendency to attach itself to the curves in the major arteries, where blood pressure is strongest. It then infiltrates through into the delicate, elastic tissue of the intima, which is easily penetrable. If the intrusion of this waste is accidental and minor, the artery self-cleaning mechanism manages to eliminate it after a time.

Dissection of diseased arteries clearly shows, in fact, traces of old, fatty deposits which have been evacuated and have healed over. But if the mixture of fatty waste continues, the drainage mechanism is soon overwhelmed. Gradually the arterial wall thickens, hardens and takes on a twisted shape which is characteristic of arteriosclerosis. As no clinical signs indicate the thickening of these internal vessels at an early stage, the invalid who does not know his own body will continue quite calmly to poison himself with his disastrous diet. Within a few years the deposit will jut out in the artery aperture. The wall necrotises.

As misfortune never comes singly, it turns out that denatured food is essentially hypercholesterolaemiant. The excess cholesterol then settles in this wound, and blood platelets then cake onto it, thus producing an atheroma, as we explained in Chapter 3.

According to Robert S. Ford, *this adulterated food theory explains a lot of matters which have become disturbing, for example, why peoples such as the Masai and the Mongols have practically no arteriosclerosis, in spite of the fact that they drink milk, eat fats and meat with a high cholesterol content, and what is more, in large quantities. Whereas the admirable Finns, who follow a regimen with a high cholesterol content, have the highest arteriosclerosis level in the world! The explanation is simple: the Masai and Mongols live close to their herds, drink their milk and eat their meat, fresh, whereas the Finns have to consume their food in what is only a fairly reasonable state of preservation, because of the long, cold winters, in the form of bread, bacon, ham, smoked fish, etc.'.*

To Ford's observations we will add two other statements in the same category, which do not involve exotic peoples, as they relate to the Americans, the Irish and the French. The latter eat as many fats as the Americans (on average 36 per cent of the daily food intake), but more saturated fatty acids and less polyunsaturated fatty acids.

French cholesterolaemia is higher than in America: 2.28g/l against 2.05g/l. However, death caused by heart disease is three times higher in the United States than in France: 300.7 per thousand against 112.4 per thousand!

Another example: the cases of Ireland and France have been compared. The French are seen to consume a little less fat than the Irish – respectively, 36 per cent and 38 per cent. However, in France, a great deal more cholesterol is consumed (in foods) than in Ireland: 495mg per day against only 309mg per day. Nevertheless, the coronary mortality indices show that there are three times as many deaths from heart attacks in Belfast as in Toulouse: 0.71 deaths per 1,000 people against 2.4!

In both cases the explanation is certainly not one of a genetic nature. It relates to the diets of these different peoples. Dr Apfelbaum, who has long been interested in this minor enigma, concludes: *'The first point (of explanation) lies in meal structure.*

 'In France, the great majority of adults eat during meals; in the United States the great majority eat when they feel like it, because food is around them all the time. And, for many Americans, snacks end up by doing away with meals. French meals consist of a number of stages starting, except on special occasions, with an averagely-exciting course such as soup, and ending, when people are already sated, with dessert. However, in the United States, desserts, sweetened drinks and minced meats take the place of meals. Also the French eat more vegetables and fruit.'

We must stress this point: hamburgers and other American 'delights' are made from products of doubtful freshness and in any case industrially treated and preserved with copious amounts of chemical products. These foods are denatured and debased.

In France, in addition to the traditionally considerable consumption of fresh fruit and vegetables, the size of the great majority of agricultural operations hardly allows for the industrial processing proper of crops (but more and more foodstuffs are being exported and imported: green beans from Africa, fruit from the Cape, or Florida, etc.). The products available are generally of satisfactory quality. The case of Ireland is similar to that of Finland: very few fresh fruit and vegetables, a lot of salted or smoked foods, or foods preserved under unsatisfactory conditions.

Noting the present fashion for American food in France among adolescents, Dr Apfelbaum warns: *'If we let them eat in the American way – that is, what they want, when they want it – it is certain that, once they become adults, the prevalence of massive obesity and premature death caused by heart disease will later reach the American levels, that is, at least three times higher than ours are today.'*

From the evidence, a diet based on fresh, wholesome, varied foods prevents or at least slows down the arteriosclerosis and arthrosic processes – apart, of course, from the existence of major hyperlipidaemia and other extra-alimentary risk factors. On the other hand, a diet based on adulterated, denatured, debased products, 'chemical' to the end, leads straight to arteriosclerosis and other degenerative illnesses. Taking stock of over thirty years' experience of dealing with fresh foods, Robert S. Ford writes:

'Few people, even among doctors, appear to understand that distinguished scientists long ago discovered that the arteries have their own cleaning system. Every deposit in the arteries follows a natural growth, maturity, withering and healing cycle; this major cleaning action can easily be seen by anyone who examines the deposits in a blocked artery, where some are quite obviously new and growing strongly, others are well-developed and others, finally, are clean craters or healed wounds. Clearly, action of this kind can result in the arteries being cleaned, if the formation of new deposits is avoided in some way.'

The only way to resorb the existing deposits and avoid the formation of new deposits is the consumption of *fresh food*. There is no scientific explanation, only repeated findings. Adulterated, preserved food increases arterial deposits; fresh food helps the body to eliminate them. The food which we recommend performs a kind of rinsing out of the arteries. There are, therefore, no definitive atheromatous deposits. Each one of us can improve the state of our arteries through healthy eating and regain a satisfactory state of health. This does not call for any drugs; it is absolutely devoid of anything unwholesome; it is not restricting – on the contrary, it is pleasant. All we need to do is to learn how to select our food and know how to prepare it and possibly preserve it. This is what we are proposing to show you in the following chapters, covering each group of foods. We begin by establishing what the body needs and in what quantities.

Chapter 5

What are our nutritional requirements?

If you wish to eat properly you need to know what your nutritional requirements are and learn the fundamentals of basic dietetics. This dietetic knowledge will help you to make the right choices with your food.

The human body needs an extraordinary variety of nutrients in order to function properly. Doctors and dieticians list these requirements under two headings, which cover the two aspects of any food: energising and nutritional.

Our body needs energy

The body burns up energy all the time, even when it is completely at rest (basal metabolism). Indeed, any activity, even if imperceptible, such as blood circulation, requires energy and *a fortiori* when we perform a piece of work. This energy is present in all foods which are, therefore, 'organic fuel' *par excellence.*

After years of research, scientists have established three categories of food, with different compositions and natures, which supply specific amounts of energy for a given amount of material:

- protids, roughly comprising meat, fish and eggs, provide 4 calories per gramme;

- glucids, which are sugars (refined sugars, but also the sugars present in most foods, including meat) also provide 4 calories per gramme;

- lipids, comprising all fats, oils and other fatty matters supply the most energy: 9 calories per gramme.

This basic data must always be taken into account for calculating the energy value of a meal. As a general rule, it has been established that distribution of the total energy to be expected from a meal must be made according to the following proportions:

- 12 per cent to 16 per cent of calories must come from protids;

- 50 per cent to 60 per cent from glucids;

- a maximum of 33 per cent of calories will be supplied by lipids.

For example, to achieve an almost ideal balance, the three daily meals, having a total energy value of 3,200 calories, must consist of:

- around 450 calories of protids, that is, 112g of meat or protid equivalent;

- around 1,750 calories of glucids, that is, 440g of sugar or the glucid equivalent;

- around 1,000 calories of lipids, that is, a little more than 90g of fatty material.

Needs vary considerably according to age, sex, weight, height and type of physical activity. As a guide, these are the averages calculated and recommended by dieticians according to these variables:

- up to 9 years of age, there are no differences between girls and boys – under 1: 112 calories per kilo of the child's body weight; between 1 and 3: 1,360 calories; between 4 and 6: 1,830 calories and, between 7 and 9: 2,190 calories.

- from 10 years onwards there is a clear sexual differentiation:
  a) girls: between 10 and 12: 2,350 calories; between 13 and 19: 2,400 calories; adult women involved in moderate physical activity: 2,000 calories; adult women involved in intense physical activity and weighing 65kg or over: 3,055 calories; during pregnancy, a supplementary supply of 150 calories per day; while lactating, a supplement of 750 calories.
  b) boys: between 10 and 12: 2,600 calories; between 13 and 19: 3,000 calories, adult men involved in moderate physical activity: 2,700 calories; adult men weighing over 75kg, involved in intense physical activity: 4,015 calories.

These figures are given as a guide. There are individual variations which are occasionally important. A doctor should be consulted, for example, by people who are very tall or, conversely, are smaller than average, or again if they have a job calling for physical effort which is considerable but not intense.

What are the connections between obesity and our energy requirements?

Normally, when needs and energy supplies are balanced, we keep the same weight over many years. Thus if my needs are 3,000 calories per day and I consume a daily food intake of exactly 3,000 calories, I will not put on a single gramme of extra weight. Unfortunately, the precise calculation of both needs and supplies cannot be produced from day to day: it would be tiresome and would make life unbearable. However, a simple weekly weight check definitely makes it possible to maintain a weight very close to the ideal.

Indeed, in one week, it is not possible to put on more than a few grammes, a kilo at the most if you obey the most elementary eating rules. This slight extra weight can easily be corrected the following week by means of minor rules which are not particularly restrictive. However, most of us nowadays refuse the slightest discipline!

The result is that they put on one, then two, then three kilos almost imperceptibly, then much more, seven, ten, fifteen kilos ... At this stage the road back to a comfortable weight is now much more difficult, because it is so much easier to put on kilos – and even up to the most 'acceptable' limit because we are happy to swallow far too much food – than to lose them, as that involves draconian restrictions, frustrations, etc.

Obesity, an important factor in arteriosclerosis and atherosclerosis, is directly related to a denatured food regimen. Fresh, balanced food prevents obesity and may even fight it if the excess weight has not reached too great proportions (under 6 to 7kg or over).

How to satisfy our protid requirements

Protids are biological substances which are high in nitrogen (1g per 6.25g of proteins) and contain amino acids which are vital for the synthesis of living tissues, hormones, enzymes and antibodies. As most of them are not manufactured, or are manufactured in insufficient quantities for the body, protid supplies are therefore absolutely essential for the normal balance and functioning of the body.

Proteins are present in foods of animal origin: meat, fish, milk and dairy products and eggs. They contain all of the requisite amino acids, but are associated with large quantities of lipids. Certain foods of vegetable origin also contain proteins: cereals, bread, lentils, dried beans and peas whose nutritional and biological value is lower than that of proteins of animal origin.

There is no protid reserve in the body which is comparable to fatty tissue for lipids and to glycogen for glucids. Hence the need to provide regular, adequate daily supplies. In addition, although caloric needs are not covered by lipids and glucids, the body covers the deficiency by transforming protids into caloric constituents, which from that time no longer play a part in the production of living tissues.

Protein requirements vary according to age and sex. Up to the age of 1 year, the supply must be 2g per kilo of the infant's body weight; between 1 and 9 the supply rises from 22g to 66g per day; during adolescence needs reach 90g per day for boys and 72g per day for girls; the male adult needs

81g per day, the female 60g per day (except when pregnant and nursing her child, when she needs 80g per day).

In certain circumstances (serious illness, major traumas) the body can reach the point of consuming its own proteins. However, a nitrogenous balance makes it possible to detect this anomaly and prevent autoconsumption (by administering glucids).

Proteins are extremely sensitive substances; they oxidise easily and are attacked by bacteria. And so the freshness requirement for all protid foods is absolutely vital.

We also need glucids

Glucids, or carbohydrates, correspond to what are generally called sugars. There are a number of varieties:

- simple sugars, which include glucose, fructose or levulose (present mainly in fruit) galactose (in gums and mucilages) and mannose, (in certain berries and vegetable seeds);

- compound sugars, which include saccharose formed by glucose and fructose (extracted from sugar cane or beet), lactose, formed by glucose and galactose (present in milk) and maltose (contained mainly in malt), formed by two molecules of glucose;

- polysaccharides, which subdivide into starch (contained in cereals and most leguminous plants), cellulose (present in fruit and vegetables and partially digestible) and glycogen.

There is a minimum supply of glucids estimated at 150g per 24 hours. This supply is vital for providing the glucose needed by certain organs which depend on glucose, such as the brain. When this minimum supply is not provided, the body is obliged to manufacture it to the detriment of protids and this can result in serious imbalances if the deficit continues over a certain period. As a general rule, in a balanced diet, glucids should represent 50 to 60 per cent of the daily total caloric supply.

Glucids play a major part in the metabolism: they, particularly glucose, supply usable energy to the cells very quickly. Glucose penetration in the cells is achieved through certain hormones, mainly insulin (lack of which causes diabetes). The liver can store part of the glucose which is not used immediately, up to 150g, in the form of glycogen. Glucids are also involved in the composition of various tissues: amino acids, (ribose) cartilage, heparin, blood group antigens, etc.

It should be noted that almost all foods contain variable quantities and qualities of one or more varieties of glucids.

What we need to know about our lipid requirements

Lipids are substances of a heterogeneous nature which are insoluble in water and roughly correspond to what we generally call fats: those contained in meat, fish, butter, vegetable oil, margarine, etc. The lipids' content varies considerably between one type of food and another.

The sources of lipids in food are classified as: a) constitutional lipids (meat and fish, eggs, milk and dairy products, oleaginous fruits); b) seasoning lipids (animal fats, such as butter, bacon, lard, goose fat; fats of vegetable origin, such as olive oil, groundnut oil, soya bean oil, etc.). It should be emphasised that vegetable foods contain very little (cereals) or practically no (fruit and vegetables) lipids. On the other hand, all foods supplying proteins contain quite large amounts of fat.

Lipids in food are made up of fatty acids. There are three varieties of fatty acids, defined by the length of their carbonaceous chain: short, medium and long fatty acids. The first two varieties are characterised by the marked ease with which they are absorbed through the intestines. They are, however, present in small amounts in normal, everyday food and ingesting them does not, therefore, have any noteworthy impact from the cholesterol and arteriosclerosis point of view.

Long-chain fatty acids are subdivided into three categories:

* 'Saturated' fatty acids: chemically, all of the carbon atoms of which they are composed are connected to hydrogen atoms; this structure provides stability when they are metabolised and cooked but gives them a hyper-triglyceridaemiant capacity; in addition, it encourages the aggregation of blood platelets. For these reasons, saturated fatty acids play an active part in the process leading to the formation of atheroma (atherogenesis).

Foods which are rich in saturated fatty acids are meat, milk, dairy products and eggs. In a balanced diet, calories of lipidic origin should never exceed 35 per cent of the total daily caloric supply. Out of this 35 per cent, saturated fatty acids should not exceed 30 to 33 per cent. Here is a quantified example, to make it possible to understand this arithmetic more easily: a total calory amount of 3,200 calories per day for an adult involved in an activity of average physical intensity; lipids will supply a maximum of 35 per cent of this, that is, 1,120 calories; in these 1,120 calories, saturated fatty acids will represent around 370 calories.

- 'Monounsaturated' fatty acids: these display the structural characteristic of being without two hydrogen atoms, which makes them chemically more reactive. Because of this they have an important biological role. They arc found in all vegetable oil and in fluid animal fats (such as goose fat). The principal monounsaturated fatty acid is oleic acid; alone it represents around 30 per cent of the fatty acids supplied by a normal, balanced diet.

- 'Polyunsaturated' fatty acids are, as their name suggests, fatty acids which are lacking a number of hydrogen atoms: because of this they are extremely reactive. They have been the subject of many research projects for decades and it has been established that they bring together, among others, all of the essential or indispensable fatty acids.

The fatty acids which the body absolutely must have, but which it is unable to synthetise, are called, linoleic acid, linolenic acid (alpha and gamma) and arachidonic acid. These acids, which were formerly called vitamin F, are involved in a number of biological processes: the growth, especially, of new-born babies, oxidating phosphorylation, enzymatic activities, permeability of the cellular membrane, (the deficiency of polyunsaturated fatty acids can result in high blood pressure), the coagulation process, capillary protection and sexual and reproductive functions, in particular.

Polyunsaturated fatty acids are present in vegetable oil in very variable quantities (see Chapter 9). The optimal requirements are a matter of dissension between the specialists, deficiencies of polyunsaturated fatty acids being extremely rare in the developed countries.

It is best, it would appear, to accept the apportionment defined in terms of calories: a third of the lipidic calories supplied by saturated fatty acids; the remaining two thirds by monounsaturated and polyunsaturated fatty acids in flexible proportions (one day a little more monounsaturated than polyunsaturated, the next day the opposite), the important consideration being to limit the supply of saturates to the proportions shown.

Cholesterol, which is very close to the lipids, and the esterified part of which is a true lipid, is present in foods of animal origin which are high in saturated fats. Normal needs in a balanced diet should not exceed 300mg per day. In practice, the average daily supply exceeds 500mg per day in the developed countries, hence the problems with arteriosclerosis and atherosclerosis referred to above.

It is also essential that our body should have water ...

Without being a food in the strict sense of the word, water is a vital element for the body. It represents 60 per cent of the body weight of an adult (between 20 and 40), this proportion falling with advancing age, and is found both in the cells (intracellular water representing 55 per cent of the total volume) and the extracellular spaces (45 per cent of the total volume). The average requirements are 2 litres per day; however, these can vary considerably in certain circumstances (ambient heat, fever, intense physical activity, etc.).

Drinking-water and table-water are classified as 'soft water', they are low in calcium and are well-suited to cooking and washing, but are liable to take in lead or zinc from the pipes, and as 'hard water', which is high in calcium but does not lend itself well to cooking and washing. Water treated with a softener loses its calcium, which it exchanges for sodium: we need to take account of this unapparent phenomenon in order to balance the sodium supply properly. French mineral waters have well-known characteristics:

- those from Vichy are particularly high in sodium and high in potassium;

- those from Vittel Grande Source, Évian, Volvic and Charrier are very low in sodium;

- those from Volvic Hépar and Badoit are high in calcium.

... and we need mineral salts, trace elements and vitamins

One preliminary general observation: the mineral salt and trace element content varies considerably according to how fresh foods are. The fresher food is, the closer its content is to the ideal. The older and more denatured a food is, the less easily-assimilable constituents it contains; sometimes, even, a food which is excessively denatured takes in toxic substances, resulting in the inevitable chemical reactions of which it is the source. Fresh food, therefore, is a guarantee of healthy, safe supplies.

We now need only to vary the foods which we eat to gain maximum benefit from what nature provides us with. In fact potassium, calcium, phosphorus, iron, chromium, chlorine, cobalt, copper, fluorine, iodine, manganese, sulphur, zinc and all vitamins are supplied by a balanced diet consisting of fresh, correctly-prepared food.

Conversely, we would draw your attention to the consumption of salt: normal requirements for an adult are around 3.5g per day. But our usual food supplies 6 to 18g per day, which is considerable and, moreover, it is dangerous (risk of high blood pressure in particular). Do not add salt automatically, without even having first tasted what is on your plate. You will rediscover how much flavour of its own each food has.

Do not forget to eat foods which are high in magnesium (dried fruits, nuts, hazelnuts and almonds, leguminous plants, cereals, cocoa) as present-day food supplies very variable amounts from one day to the next, depending on the menu, so that deficiencies are not altogether uncommon.

A nutritional requirement not to be overlooked: fibres

Food fibres are substances of vegetable origin which form part of the composition and structure of a large number of vegetables. With their heterogeneous structures they stand up quite well to the digestion process. They are made up of polysaccharides: cellulose, pectin and lignite. Of the celluloses, some are partially digestible, but their caloric supply is negligible. Lignites completely escape digestion and therefore have no calorific value.

Fibres, however, play an important part in nutrition. On the one hand they form a kind of 'ballast' which facilitates and accelerates transit through the intestines, thus preventing constipation. On the other, by increasing the volume of the faecal bolus, they contribute to the maintenance of the intestinal muscle structure: a diet regularly containing appropriate amounts of vegetable fibre effectively combats 'lazy' intestines, that is, the slackening of their muscle structure.

Finally, and this is not the least of their advantages, fibres absorb water and fats, including cholesterol, thereby reducing even the lipid supply, whose overabundance in our societies has been emphasised.

However, we need to be sensible, as always. Food which is too rich in fibre (by adding excessive amounts of bran, for example) can have harmful effects. It can cause diarrhoea, excessively reduce the resorption of lipids, bile, mineral salts such as potassium, calcium, magnesium and certain water-soluble vitamins. Eating fruit and vegetables in reasonable quantities and, most importantly, regularly, at every meal, is quite sufficient to supply the body with the 'ballast' which it requires.

The sources of dietary fibres are mainly:

- non-digestible fibres: whole cereals, wheat bran, cabbages, cauliflowers, tomatoes, etc;

- partially-digestible fibres: all fresh fruits and vegetables, especially apples, pears, citrus fruit; vegetables and dried fruit are also high in cellulose but they should be eaten in moderation.

One important observation: the freshness of fruit or vegetables determines the quality of the fibres which it contains. The fresher food is, the better its fibres help transit through the intestines, without causing irritation. The older food is, the more its fibres are tough and irritating for the intestinal wall. It is vital to take this into account when choosing fruits and vegetables in the market.

Now that you are properly acquainted with your needs and the various commodities which satisfy these, we shall examine the most common foods together, those that you eat or have eaten regularly, and we shall see what you need to select to clean your arteries.

Chapter 6

Meat, poultry, eggs and your arteries

As a rule, meats and meat products do not present any special hygiene problems in this country. Veterinary inspections are performed on the premises of breeders of animals for slaughter, where the animals are actually reared, in order to detect any animal diseases which may be transmittable to man.

Overall, therefore, the risks of having meat in the food chain which has suffered bacterial or microbial contamination are minute. But these measures are not 100 per cent reliable. For example, the detection of cysticercus, (a parasite responsible for cysticcrcosis, which is a serious infection for people) is not always simple and usually can be achieved only in easily-accessible regions. Moreover, health inspection does not provide any information on the nutritional quality and value of a certain piece of meat.

But there is worse to come: contamination of meat by chemical products. This can arise following the administration, during rearing, of substances dangerous to animals intended for slaughter: hormones (to fatten them up more quickly, artificially, by water retention) and antibiotics. These production methods, which are now prohibited or subjected to draconian regulations in very limited cases, were at the root of the scandals which hit the headlines in recent years. Although the great majority of breeders have stopped using them there are, unfortunately, still a few well-known cases of backsliding on the part of unscrupulous individuals.

As the detection of the substances in question is not a simple matter, it may be thought that a fairly considerable number of frauds go undetected. Here again, vigilance exercised by the consumer, who should be wary of products offered at ridiculous prices or under dubious conditions, will be the best bulwark against abuses.

Another cause of the indirect chemical pollution of fresh meat is connected with the feed given to livestock. The excessive use of pesticides in agriculture (we shall come back to this in the chapter on fruit and vegetables) has resulted in grass or hay being contaminated by pesticides, which later appear in the fat of the animals, and so passed on to the consumers.

What does meat provide us with?

The nutritional value of meat is extremely variable from one type to another, and even in the same animal from one part to another. The information that can be given relates, therefore, only to averages, which should be considered as values which are merely indicative and not official. From the nutritional aspect the protid, lipid, glucid, mineral salt, vitamin and water content, mainly, will be considered.

Meat, in general, contains around 20 per cent protein – less than cheese (30 per cent), more than fish (14 per cent) and eggs (13 per cent). In the meat most commonly consumed we find, before cooking:

- 22 per cent protein for game and duck;

- 21 per cent for chicken and horsemeat;

- 20 per cent for liver (ox, mutton, pork) and turkey;

- 19 per cent for veal;

- 17 per cent for beef and mutton;

- 16 per cent for pork and lamb.

The lipid content in meat also varies considerably, according to a number of criteria: breed, cut, age, sex, fattening, type of food, work done by the animal before slaughter.

Lean meat contains less than 10 per cent lipids (horsemeat 2 per cent, game 3 per cent, liver 5 per cent, brains 9 per cent); medium-fat meat (including grilling meat), provides between 10 and 20 per cent lipids; fat meat, such as pork and goose, for example, between 20 and 30 per cent. The type of culinary preparation can considerably modify the lipids rate in food when it is ready to be ingested, depending on the substances added to it.

From our standpoint, the cholesterol content of meat must be given full attention. Indeed, certain cuts and, in particular, offal are very high in cholesterol, and eating these must, therefore, be controlled, or even completely avoided for people who have even moderate cholesterolaemia.

The following are the average contents, expressed in mg, for 100g of fresh meat:

- calf brain: 1,810;

- calf and mutton kidney: 400;

- pork kidney: 365;

- pork liver: 340;

- calf liver: 314;

- ox liver: 265;

- calf's sweetbread: 225;

- chicken: 100;

- calf: 84;

- mutton: 77;

- beef: 67;

- pork: 60.

These contents are for fresh cuts, before cooking. The culinary preparation method may increase the indicative value, in particular if substances which themselves are high in cholesterol are added.

Meat contains very few glucids (1 to 1.5 per cent at the most), in the form of glycogen, which shortly after slaughter is transformed into lactic acid.

Important observation

All of the information which we have just examined is applicable to animals for slaughter which have been reared under normal conditions. However, industrial production methods tend to denature the quality of meat by the use of methods which are hardly in accordance with the animals' normal food and way of life.

It is, therefore, essential to be demanding as regards the quality of the meat we buy and to find out, by questioning the butcher or the poulterer, about the source of the meat we are buying, and the way the animals were reared.

A piece of simple, practical advice: make the most of your holidays in the country to purchase farm products, such as chickens and eggs in particular, and buy your meat from the local butcher, who usually obtains his supplies from farmers in the area. You will appreciate the delicacy, superiority and fine quality of these fresh, natural products.

Prepared meat damages your arteries

Apart from the fresh meat sold in butchers' and poulterers' shops, a large number of meat products, differently prepared and presented are available. This always involves non-fresh food, usually from animals killed some months, even some years, before and preserved by various techniques and processes.

This type of food, eaten in enormous quantities, has irrefutable arteriosclerosis risks, sometimes even more serious dangers to health (cancers). We will now examine them from this angle.

Hung game: to be avoided at all costs. Hung game should be banished from your diet. It presents risks not only of poisoning but also of contamination by parasites. You should, therefore, eat only fresh game.

Cooked meats are not, of course, recommended.
Cooked meats are meat by-products, generally made from pork, whose essential characteristic as regards nutrition is their extremely high level of saturated fatty acid lipids and cholesterol. One could well say that they are exceptionally atherogenous foods and therefore should be excluded completely from the diet of any person suffering from hypercholesterolaemia; even those with normal cholesterolaemia should eat them only sparingly, even frugally.

Thus the cooked ham, although supposed to be 'lean', contains over 22g/100g of saturated lipids and 55mg/100g of cholesterol. Moreover, a number of chemical substances are added, namely nitrited salt and sugar, and often polyphosphates, intended to combat microbial and bacterial proliferation. These substances do not, of course, remain inert and degrade the proteins and lipids, giving rise to considerable fatty waste. Moreover, these various additives do not prevent putrefaction from taking place on occasion: iridescent bluish or greenish traces seen on certain hams are the sign of microbial activity.

Raw ham, produced by drying, is hardly more wholesome. For only 15g/100g of proteins, it provides 30.5g of lipids (saturated fatty acids), 70mg of cholesterol and 50mg of uric acid. In addition, contamination by insect larvae is not unknown.

Pâtés are made from pieces or the remains of fresh, unused pieces of offal, minced and cooked, with eggs, milk or jelly and amylaceous substances added. The quality of the products used is difficult for the public health services to control. On average, pâtés supply 42 to 45g/100g of saturated lipids and over 90mg of cholesterol! Liver pâtés are even worse: produced using pork or chicken liver and various fats, they supply 450 calories per 100g, 45 to 50g of saturated lipids and a . . . maximum dose of cholesterol! Raw pig liver contains 350mg/100g of cholesterol.

Liver pâté is a traditional preparation, a prestige food, produced using hypertrophied liver from an overfed goose, seasoned with various ingredients. From the simple physiological point of view it will be noted that the flesh used is already an abnormal product. In addition, like the liver from all animals, it has a very high cholesterol content. It is, therefore, a product to be avoided entirely.

Sausages and slicing sausage, whatever their origin or method of preparation may be, are also antidietetic products, containing large amounts of lipids, cholesterol and chemical additives which are harmful to some degree (namely the colorants). It would be wise, therefore, to avoid them, the more so because they do not provide any worthwhile nourishment which is not found in fresh meat products.

No tinned meats . . .
Tinned meats have lost their vitamins and contain a large number of preservatives, additives and colorants of uncertain innocuousness. They also contain an excessive amount of sodium. Eating these is strictly advised against for those who wish to clean their arteries.

. . . or smoked meats . . .
Smoked meats contain polycyclic hydrocarbons, such as 3-4 benzopyrene, a well-known carcinogen. Like all 'non-fresh' products, these meats should also be avoided.

... or salt meats

Salt meats (that is, preserved by salting), should also be avoided. Fortunately, they are disappearing gradually from our dietary habits. They are dangerous because of the nitrates which they contain and which change into nitrites in your stomach.

To sum up, only fresh meat, of good quality, should be eaten if you do not wish to harm your arteries.

A special protid food: eggs

Eggs from most birds have been used for food by man for centuries. However, the chicken egg is the one which, by far, is most often eaten all over the world. It is a valuable food: for a relatively low caloric value (160 calories per 100g of fresh eggs, therefore 80 to 90 calories per egg), it provides an almost complete range of nutrients which are essential for the body. The white consists of albumins which are high in vital amino acids. The yolk contains albumins, lipids, mineral salts and vitamins.

A complete new-laid egg contains specifically, per 100g:

- 0.6g of glucids; 11.5g of lipids, including (unfortunately) 450mg of cholesterol; 12.8g of proteins;

- mineral salts in abundance: 208mg of phosphorus; 54mg of calcium; 138mg of potassium; 135mg of chlorine; 130mg of sodium; 188mg of sulphur; 11mg of magnesium and, in much smaller amounts, a considerable number of trace elements;

- vitamins: A: 0.34mg (it should be noted that the yolk contains many more: 0.98mg/100g); B2: 0.34mg; B6: 0.36mg; D: 0.1mg.

Eggs, which are almost a complete food, must always be eaten very fresh. They must come from free-range chickens, fed naturally. Eggs from chickens fed in battery units have a very fragile shell and a yolk which breaks easily in the pan, unlike eggs from free-range chickens, whose yolks are firm and form a compact mass of brilliant orange-yellow. Old eggs have a dull appearance.

The egg is, however, a food which is forbidden for people suffering from even mild hypercholesterolaemia. For individuals with normal cholesterolaemia it can usefully replace meat and fish once or twice a week – if it is, in fact, fresh (laid less than forty-eight hours previously) and organic (free-range chickens). Its digestibility varies according to the way it is cooked and to individual tolerances.

Observation: an egg can carry salmonella germs if it has been laid on contaminated ground and especially if it is old and insufficiently cooked. Cases of salmonellosis are usually confined to regions where the disease is rife in its endemic state. There is, therefore, no cause for alarm, in spite of the series of cases reported in Great Britain sometime ago. It will be noted, on the other hand, that duck eggs are more often contaminated than chicken eggs. Because of this it is recommended that they should be eaten only hard, that is, well-cooked.

PRACTICAL ADVICE

Meat, poultry and eggs form one of the main sources of proteins in normal, healthy eating in Europe and in the developed countries. In order to prevent and restrict progressive clogging of the arteries, leading to arteriosclerosis and atherosclerosis, care must be taken to:

1. Eat only absolutely fresh meat, poultry and eggs.

2. Limit the daily energy supply amount obtained from protids to 10-12 per cent.

3. Strictly limit, or give up, depending on each individual cholesterol level, cooked meats, offal, giblets, preserved, dried, salted and smoked meats, meat dishes prepared industrially.

4. Endeavour to vary supplies: do not eat only one kind of meat, for example beef; eat all kinds of meat (for grilling, stewing, braising).

5. Observe dietetic cooking rules, about which we shall talk later.

6. Eggs are forbidden in all cases of hypercholesterolaemia, even mild ones; on the other hand, they are recommended at the rate of two eggs per week on average, for normal cholesterolaemia.

Chapter 7

Fish and seafood are good for your arteries

Fish and other seafood are another very valuable, relatively plentiful, source of proteins and mineral salts. However, only a limited number of species form part of the normal human diet. Out of the 12,000 or so species listed, that is, as many as all the other species of vertebrates together, a few dozen at the most are eaten regularly.

Composition and nutritive constituents of the flesh of fresh fish

With regard to cholesterol content, excepting the liver, fish contains less than meat: 20 to 70mg/100g of flesh, against 70 to 80mg/100g of meat. It is, therefore, a more useful food for preventing hypercholesterolaemia.

Fish are classified, according to their lipids content, into fish known as meagre (content less then 5 per cent, such as whiting, John Dory, skate, sole, hake and sea bream ...) semi-oily fish (content between 5 and 10 per cent, such as sardine, grey mullet, red mullet ...) and oily fish (content over 10 per cent, such as mackerel, tuna and eel).

Fish flesh contains very few glucids. This is why it is always recommended that it should be eaten with starchy foods (rice, potato, etc.) in order to produce a well-balanced meal.

To summarise, the flesh of fresh fish is a first-rate food, superior in many respects to meat. Eating it regularly may help to regulate and stabilise the blood cholesterol level.

The exceptional food qualities of fish are understood to relate to the freshly-caught product, eaten a few hours later. We would, therefore, stress this 'freshness' factor. But very often, before it reaches our table, fish has undergone various preservative treatments which modify its nutritional characteristic quite profoundly.

Preservation using refrigeration is healthy
Freezing and deep-freezing of sea food is now well-managed, ensuring perfect hygiene in most cases.

Although these procedures change the proteins, the nutritive value of the fish is hardly impaired.

Drying and salt-drying: to be avoided
Protein, fat and mineral concentrations increase sharply in dried fish: 100g of dried cod produces 322 calories, against just 70 calories for fresh cod! In addition, there is a significant loss of vitamins.

This preservation method is no longer justified nowadays in the developed countries.

As regards salt fish (tuna, sardine, anchovy, mackerel) and certain of these when dried (cod . . .) they are advised against completely in any healthy, balanced diet.

Smoked fish: only occasionally
Although the smoking technique has been improved, eating

smoked salmon, or kippers, is most inadvisable. You can, of course, eat these every two or three months, bearing in mind that they are something to be avoided.

Prohibited: tinned foods

In all instances, analysis of the content of the tin reveals quite a high number of chemical substances.

Moreover, this kind of product, which should be used only in emergency or certain non-repetitive circumstances (picnics, travelling ...) certainly has no place on the everyday family table and must be proscribed if you want to protect your arteries.

The same applies to semi-preserved foods such as anchovy fillets, herrings in oil or rollmops.

Observation: We shall not dwell on other seafood products, in particular shellfish and molluscs, which are eaten in moderation when in season.

One piece of advice, however: avoid gathering these in the wild at the coast, while on holiday, obtain your supplies from professional fishermen.

Preferably, do not eat shellfish heads, these are often very high in cholesterol.

People with hypercholesterolaemia above 2.5 must not eat certain varieties of oyster, which contain up to 300mg/100g of cholesterol, nor mussels, which again contain 150mg/100g.

PRACTICAL ADVICE

1. Eat fresh fish at least twice a week, preferably meagre and prepared in a court bouillon, or meunière, using very little fat.

2. Eliminate dried, salted, smoked or tinned fish.

3. Eat seafood in moderation, avoiding shellfish heads, which are high in cholesterol.

Chapter 8

What you need to know about milk and dairy products

Of all protid food products, this is the least expensive, the most plentiful, available everywhere, fresh or prepacked in various ways, full-cream, semi-skimmed or skimmed.

Its cholesterol content is not, however, negligible: 10mg per 100ml. Because of this, full-cream milk is forbidden in all cases of hypercholesterolaemia: it must be replaced by liquid skimmed milk, which provides all the benefits of milk without the disadvantages.

Butter and cream may be eaten uncooked

Butter and cream, including the so-called 'low-fat' presentations, where the consumer pays dearly for added water, must be eaten in great moderation in the diet of people suffering from hypercholesterolaemia, even mildly.

As for butter cooked at a high temperature – and *a fortiori* 'brown' butter sauce – this is strictly forbidden. Uncooked butter (20 to 40g per day maximum), remains a not unimportant source of the vitamin supply (in particular A).

We would, however, now like to give you a recipe which is very easy to follow and makes it possible to eat butter without the risks presented by commercial products; this should be followed by everyone, cholesterol or no cholesterol ...

Clarified butter is a traditional method which makes it possible to purify butter by removing its most toxic, indigestible constituents. It is prepared as follows:

Use unsalted butter, which you place in a thick-bottomed pan. Leave the butter to melt gently. A froth then forms on the surface and this will tend to precipitate to the bottom of the pan as a deposit which you can skim off from time to time.

Allow to boil on a very low heat. When the butter turns more golden, cooking should stop. (At the bottom of the pan the deposits will be starting to caramelise.)

Pass through a very fine sieve: a compress with a number of thicknesses, or a fine cotton cloth, are quite suitable.

The whole operation takes around thirty-five minutes for 750g of butter.

Butter clarified in this way is then a much more stable product than ordinary butter. It does not turn rancid and, in summer, it is possible to leave it out at ambient temperature.

It keeps very well in an earthenware vessel. Its changed taste brings hazelnuts to mind. You can use it like ordinary butter, in your cooking or on your bread.

Choose fresh cheeses

Besides the fresh white cheeses available, shops now stock skimmed milk cheeses with 0 per cent fats: these are the only ones which can be eaten by persons suffering from hypercholesterolaemia.

Although it is extremely high in mineral salts, particularly calcium and phosphorus, cheese is not a vital food, more a food for enjoyment. In fact, the sustenance which it supplies can be found in a number of other types of food.

Apart from the stringent restrictions linked to the existence of hypercholesterolaemia, the moderate consumption of all cheeses is permitted, according to personal taste. 'Mature' cheeses which have ripened over a long period, however, are not recommended. As Robert S. Ford has stressed, the bacterial colonies active in these cheeses *'transform part of the fat in the milk into fatty acids which, combined with calcium, form insoluble calcareous cakes, rather like those powdery marks which you can see all around the bath when it has dried after someone has had a bath. This material has been found by a number of scientists in blocked arteries, in much higher amounts than cholesterol'.*

PRACTICAL ADVICE

1. In all cases of hypercholesterolaemia, even mild ones, full-cream milk, butter, cream and all cheeses (fresh, fermented or in spread form) should be proscribed. Only skimmed milk and dairy products containing 0 per cent fat are permitted.

2. In the diet of a healthy adult, skimmed milk should be preferred, preferably pasteurised, low-fat dairy products and a moderate intake of uncooked butter (never cooked) and 'young' fermented cheeses, with a hard crust, pressed and cooked (Gruyère, Emmenthal, Comté, parmesan, etc.) or pressed and uncooked (Dutch, cantal, Saint-Paulin, Bonbel, reblochon, etc.).

3. Fresh, pasteurised full-cream milk and dairy products made from full-cream milk (fresh or otherwise) are foods which are recommended for children and adolescents (unless there is an inability to tolerate these), pregnant women or nursing mothers, older people or those suffering from decalcification. They are not suitable for people with arterial problems.

4. In general, the ingestion of dairy products must be supplemented by fresh vegetables, particularly those with green leaves such as salads, in order to balance the meal. All meals based exclusively on milk or dairy products must be excluded.

Chapter 9

Fats and oils, friends and enemies of your arteries

If we except that butter, which if eaten uncooked and in moderate amounts may be recommended for people who have normal cholesterolaemia, most animal and vegetable oils and fats can be considered as being major suppliers of cholesterol and other fatty waste which builds up in the arteries.

It is mainly overindulgence and the disastrous way in which we consume these products that should be called to account. Indeed, these products, when they are natural, that is, not subjected to chemical or other processes which denature and debase them, have extremely valuable nutritional qualities and virtues. However, the consumer usually finds only hyperrefined products in the market, denatured and made practically unassimilable by the body.

To these disadvantages is added ignorance of elementary dietetic and nutritional rules on the part of the consumer. The result has been described by Robert S. Ford in the following horrendous picture:

'Most oils and fats sold in the shops are highly refined by heat and chemical treatments, which stabilise them to such an extent that they are not easily assimilated by the body and so remain in

the blood, mingling so horribly that nowadays, when an autopsy is performed, we find great masses of yellow oil in the heart cavities and in the major arteries, in place of blood!

It is appropriate, therefore, in order to prevent any arteriosclerosis or atherosclerosis processes, to be aware of the nature of the materials and oils in general use and the potential dangers involved in thoughtlessly ingesting them.

1. Animal fats are all harmful

These fats, coming from pork (lard), beef or marine life are strictly advised against in a natural, healthy diet.

However, and if you want to be able to eat them, because you like them or for some other reason, this is what you can do: buy internal animal fat, which must be irreproachably fresh, from an abattoir or butcher, wash it, cut it into small pieces or thin strips, and then dry it very carefully; pack it into a number of small, suitable plastic bags and put it into the freezer. When required, remove one of the small bags, (avoid handling them too much, hence the need to divide the pieces of fat into a number of bags) and put the small pieces of well-preserved fat to melt in the oven. The melted fat must be used only once, as it deteriorates very quickly.

2. Vegetable fats should also be avoided

In Europe, consumption of vegetable fats is practically unknown, and we can say with great pleasure: 'fortunately!' ...

Coconut fat and palm fat are exceptionally atherogenous.

They are to be excluded from all normal diets. Better still, the consumer should avoid any industrial food products containing them. Unfortunately, however, their presence is not often mentioned.

3. What vegetable oil should we choose?

What will guide our choice is the polyunsaturated fatty acids content of the various oils commonly used and available to us: the more of these the oil contains, the better it will suit us.

Groundnut oil
This oil, which is widely used and is relatively balanced and stable, can be used for frying. It is, however, forbidden in all cases of hypercholesterolaemia, as it has a relatively high saturated fatty acids content (21 per cent) and is low in polyunsaturated fatty acids (22 per cent).

Rape-seed oil
This oil is suitable for ordinary use. However, it is advised against in all cases of hypercholesterolaemia, in spite of its low saturated fatty acids content (7.5 per cent), as it has only 32 per cent polyunsaturated fatty acids.

Corn oil
Corn oil is low in saturated acids (13.5 per cent) and high in polyunsaturated fatty acids (56 per cent). It is, therefore, recommended for hypercholesterolaemia diets and in the prevention of arteriosclerosis.

Walnut oil
This oil is obtained by cold pressing and is often used in its

pure form. It is, therefore, a natural product which has not been adulterated and which also has a very pleasant taste.

Its high polyunsaturated fatty acids content (71 per cent) makes it very delicate and difficult to keep. It must be consumed uncooked (seasoning).

It is one of the best oils for people suffering from hypercholesterolaemia; it even appears to fight the atherogenesis process.

Olive oil

This oil, which is used world-wide for general purposes, has an indisputable nutritional value. According to certain specialists it exercises a protective action on the vascular system in general and on the arterial walls in particular. Eaten in moderation, preferably uncooked as a seasoning, by individuals with normal cholesterolaemia, it is, therefore, beneficial. However, it is advised against for people with hypercholesterolaemia.

Grapeseed oil

This oil is more difficult to find in the shops, which is a great pity because if we had any oil to recommend in hypercholesterolaemia diets, it would undoubtedly be this one (73 per cent polyunsaturated fatty acids).

Grapeseed oil has a pleasant taste and keeps well but is, however, fairly delicate and should be consumed only uncooked.

Soya bean oil

This is a particularly delicate oil, which explains why its packaging is often strengthened in order to avoid the risk of oxidation.

In hypercholesterolaemia diets it is useful, especially when consumed uncooked and in small quantities.

4. Margarine is hydrogenated, and therefore artificial

Let us be clear about this: margarines are products which have been created artificially by the food industries and consist of water (16 per cent average), various animal and vegetable fatty material in very variable proportions, and additives.

The fats and oils used in this mixture are all hydrogenated, even interesterified, either partially or completely: they are hyperrefined and are therefore denatured products.

The manufacturers are the ones who decide the fatty acid, aromatic additive and colorant content and that of other chemical preservative or palatability products. Advertising campaigns undertake to persuade the customer to eat these kinds of fatty cocktails ...

The consumption of margarines or foods containing them is strongly advised against (there are plenty of natural fats and their prices are low). It is strictly forbidden for persons suffering from hypercholesterolaemia and atheromatous deposits.

PRACTICAL ADVICE

1. Animal and vegetable fats, with the exception of fresh butter, should never be included in a normal, balanced diet; they are forbidden in all cases of cholesterolaemia and arterial deposits.

2. Vegetable oils recommended are those which have a high polyunsaturated fatty acids content (grapeseed, walnut, sunflower, soya bean and corn oil). Nevertheless they should be consumed in moderate quantities, uncooked and in seasoning. They should not be used for frying or any other cooking.

3. Vegetable oils which are high in saturated fatty acids (groundnut and rape-seed) are forbidden for persons who have a high cholesterol level and are advised against for everyone.

4. Do not under any circumstances use margarine.

Chapter 10

Fresh vegetables and pulses will help you to clean out your arteries

For thousands of years, fresh vegetables and pulses, together with fruit, have provided the basic essentials of the human diet. Indeed meat, fish and other foods of animal origin were scarce and expensive. It could be said that our body is particularly well-adapted to eating and transforming vegetables, which provide it with energy, essential nutrients, (mineral salts, trace elements, vitamins ...) and non-nutritional elements, cellulose and fibres, which are essential for the digestive tract to function efficiently.

The qualities of vegetables are even more directly dependent on their state of freshness, on the period which has elapsed between the time they were harvested and the time they are eaten. In addition, the composition of these foods always translates the chemical composition of the soils on which the vegetables have grown (the part played by manuring, using organic or chemical fertilisers).

We therefore recommend that you should select your vegetables according to the season during which they naturally come to maturity in this climate. Choose a good cabbage in winter in preference to green beans or tomatoes which have neither taste nor nutritional value, manufactured artificially under glass, with the massive use of fertilisers whose chemical constituents accelerate the destruction of their tissues. Choose what are known as organic products (which are, incidentally, available more and more readily in the shops), even though they may be a little more expensive.

Regular daily consumption of fresh vegetables, in sufficient amounts, is one of the best preventative measures against degenerative diseases of the arteries and against deposits in the arteries and joints. However, individuals suffering from calcification problems must be careful not to eat acid vegetables (spinach, Chinese cabbage or rhubarb) containing oxalic acid, which is unfavourable to the assimilation of calcium.

One further piece of advice: it is absolutely vital to vary the types of vegetables consumed and not to neglect any of them: root vegetables, tubers, green vegetables, leaf vegetables, pulses (especially in the cold seasons, at the rate of once or twice a week to replace meat dishes). This is the best way of ensuring adequate coverage of the body's calcium, potassium, sodium, phosphorus, iron, magnesium, minerals and trace elements requirements and those of all vitamins (except B12 and E).

This is not good news for those who are always looking out for ways for saving time, but frozen vegetables, and especially tinned vegetables, are strongly advised against for the normal everyday diet (exceptions are, of course, permissible ...) and are actually totally prohibited for people who want to improve the condition of their arteries.

Chapter 11

Fresh fruit, dried fruit, tinned fruit and jam

Fruit is still an invaluable food in all latitudes and for all nations. Even mythologies have seized upon it – evidence, if this were needed, of its vital necessity for mankind (for example, Adam and Eve's famous apple). From a strictly nutritional point of view, fruit, which is a plant food *par excellence*, can be compared to vegetables, but differs significantly from them in its chemical composition. More than vegetables it needs to be eaten fresh and usually raw (whereas the latter almost always need to be cooked or at least seasoned).

It can be said that of all the foods most frequently consumed by mankind, fruit is the one which is the most natural food, the most pleasant to eat just as it is, the nearest approach to the nutritional ideal.

1. What does fresh fruit provide you with?

Fresh fruit is fairly close to fresh vegetables with regard to its composition. The calorific supply is to a considerable extent the same, weight for weight, except for a few types such as avocados, bananas, grapes and fresh figs, for example.

Moreover, fruit is very low in sodium, whereas it supplies high levels of potassium: it is recommended, therefore, in all low-salt diets, and regular consumption of it by healthy individuals is a means of preventing high blood pressure. Dried fruits are, of course, more concentrated as regards minerals and they also supply higher amounts of iron than those found in meat products, fish, eggs and dairy products. However, be wary of the high calorific value and cholesterol content of these foods!

Fresh and dried fruit also provides a good number of trace elements, in not inconsiderable amounts. They therefore contribute to the general nutritional balance.

But of all the benefits obtained from a diet high in a variety of fruit, the vitamin supply, in particular vitamin C, is what the general public best knows. Quite rightly! Indeed, essentially, fruit is no higher in vitamins than vegetables. But while the vitamins in vegetables are destroyed, in part, by storing, cooking and preparation conditions, the vitamins in fruit eaten fresh, as it stands, lose very little: fruit is, therefore, the best source of vitamins, at levels which at times are very valuable.

There is another reason, which is more scientific and significant, and which should encourage us to eat fruit every day: the vitamin C which it contains, especially that in 'acid' fruit such as citrus fruit, is associated with substances called 'bioflavonoids'; bioflavonoids have the exceptional property of strengthening the resistance of blood vessels, in particular the arteries. Eating fresh fruit is not, therefore, merely a very pleasant way of supplying the body with essential nutritional elements, but also an effective way of preventing degeneration of the blood vessels. In this respect, the grape appears to be the fruit which is richest in bioflavonoids, even though its vitamin C content is relatively modest. We should never detract from making a habit of having a course of grape treatment every year!

2. Take careful note of these observations

As well as ascorbic acid, fruit contains other vitamins at levels which are sometimes very valuable.

- Certain fruit, such as citrus fruit, apples and bananas may be stored naturally over fairly long periods. But beware! The various chemical products used by growers to treat fruit finally, over a period, penetrate its flesh in depth and therefore pass into the body after ingestion. Washing fruit, even very carefully, will not prevent this poisoning, which is all the more dangerous as it goes almost unnoticed! Consequently, care should always be taken to buy, and store for a few weeks, only untreated fruit.

- A large number of people believe that they are 'eating naturally' by crunching into fruit without any other precautions. This is a serious mistake, because even if this fruit has not been treated it has been touched by hands of doubtful cleanliness; moreover, storing it near to, or even in contact with, other treated products can lead to contamination.

  It is, therefore, essential to wash fruit and dry it carefully, which will avoid you having stomatitis, gastritis and other stomach troubles.

- Certain fruit, especially grapes, strawberries, raspberries and other berries, is given special chemical treatments.

Products used in this way concentrate at the base of the grape or berry. It is best, therefore, to wash them under the tap, as just soaking them is not enough to remove a major part of the chemical products.

3. What should be our attitude to dried fruit, tinned fruit and jam?

The consumption of dried fruit with high concentrations of sugar, minerals and vegetable fibre is certainly not advised against if it is no more than reasonable and occasional. Eating it more regularly and intensively can cause a number of digestive problems, even hypermineralisation, in individuals who are sensitive to it. Here again, everything is a question of balance and moderation!

Tinned fruit is of only low nutritional interest. On the one hand, the cooking process causes it to lose a large part of its vitamins; on the other, the mineral elements disappear from the flesh of the fruit and are found in the hyperglucidic syrup in which undesirable chemical combinations, even though these are not harmful, may take place. This is why it is not recommended in any healthy diet, particularly for ailing arteries.

Clearly, fruit in jam, jellies or marmalade is very low in vitamins and mineral salts and contains fairly large amounts of additives, taste modifiers and other chemical preservatives. Consumption of these, therefore, is of small nutritional interest. Although they may not be proscribed, consumption should at least be watched and they should be limited as much as possible.

PRACTICAL ADVICE

1. Regularly eat at least two pieces of fresh seasonal fruit every day.

2. Before fresh fruit is eaten it should always be washed carefully and wiped with a clean cloth.

3. Dried fruit supplies important amounts of mineral salts and vegetable fibre. However, consumption of it should be very moderate; it is not recommended for those suffering from dyspepsia.

4. Jam, jellies and marmalade are hypercalorific and of scant nutritional interest. Strictly limit the amounts you eat. Opt for stewed fruit and the juice of fresh fruit.

Chapter 12

What kinds of cereal and flour should you eat?

Dietary grains are all fruits of grasses and are almost always eaten dried (grain) after milling. In the developed countries, mainly wheat, rice and, to a lesser extent, barley, rye, maize and buckwheat are now consumed. However, for thousands of years, cereals have supplied the essential part of mankind's food. It is only since the nineteenth century that other foods, which have become more plentiful as a result of new production methods, have gradually reduced the share held by cereals, before replacing them in Western Europe and North America.

Cereals each have their own properties

In order to give a general idea of the essential properties of the different cereals it should be remembered that:

- wheat and rice are the best balanced as regards varied nutritional elements; they are particularly suitable for people with anaemia, asthenia and essential mineral deficiencies and for outdoor workers; rice also has hypotensive properties;

- barley is restorative; it encourages calcification of the skeleton (hence its interest in the diets of children and adolescents) and fortifies the nervous cells;

- rye fluidifies the blood and in particular keeps the arteries supple: it is, therefore, particularly recommended for individuals who are predisposed to, or already suffering from, an arteriosclerosis syndrome;

- oat, which is a cold country cereal, is a stimulant and tonic; it is recommended for people with hypothyroid and asthenia and for lymphatic complaints;

- corn exerts a moderating action on the functions of the thyroid;

- buckwheat, a cereal rich in vitamin P, fortifies the blood vessels; it has the same indications as rye.

To sum up, therefore, it can be stated that it is not by chance that cereals have been supplying the basic essentials of food for mankind for centuries. However, they cannot under any circumstances represent the sole source of food.

Thus we should give up industrial white flour and preparations (bread, pastries, white rice, etc.) made from this flour, which has been deprived of its essential nutrients. The consumer must seek out cereals and cereal preparations produced in accordance with the traditional growing method known as the organic method; we should eat whole cereals and cereal products made from whole cereals, high in fibre, minerals and vitamins ...

PRACTICAL ADVICE

1. Eat all kinds of cereals regularly, in a number of forms, in moderate amounts: 100 to 150g per day on average.

2. Eat only farinaceous products obtained from 'whole' grain and grown using traditional methods (without chemical fertilisers or pesticides).

3. Do not hesitate to add a small spoonful of bran to culinary preparations such as soup, etc., if bran can comfortably be tolerated (no intestinal irritation).

Chapter 13

Our sugar requirements

Sugar belongs to the glucids group. Household sugar consists mainly of saccharose. It is extracted from beet and sugar cane (respectively 45 and 55 per cent of world production).

In its various forms sugar is the major source of the daily calorie intake in the human diet. It is present in all foods, both animal and vegetable in origin. We shall concern ourselves here only with domestic sugar in powdered, lump or slab form and with culinary preparations which include large quantities of it (such as pastries, confectionery and other sweets). Are they dangerous to health? Do they have a part in the arteriosclerosis process?

Firstly it is appropriate to call to mind two fundamental concepts: domestic sugar is sugar which can quickly be assimilated, that is, it enters the bloodstream after a very short period; conversely, sugars which are assimilated slowly and are contained mainly in starchy and farinaceous foods, etc., must undergo a number of transformations in the body before they can be mobilised and used. On the other hand, any excess amounts of sugar (supply exceeding requirements) are systematically transformed into reserve lipids, fat; therefore excessive consumption of sugar always translates into an accumulation of reserve fat and therefore into obesity.

It can be seen that excessive consumption of sugar, even by a healthy person, can trigger off an arteriosclerosis process by means of the 'obesity' factor.

For someone already suffering from arteriosclerosis there is a grave danger in eating a large amount of sugar at any one time. Indeed, as refined sugar is assimilated quickly, it is mobilised by the body within an hour of ingestion. However, a massive increase in the blood sugar level results in a rise in 'osmotic pressure', which can result in the bursting of the most fragile capillaries; the threat of a heart attack or stroke is multiplied by ten!

This is why eating rapidly-assimilable sugar is prohibited for those with arterial problems (and for diabetics, of course).

We often hear it said that brown sugar is less harmful than white sugar. What is the truth in this? The consumer believes that brown sugar is always produced from cane. This is not correct: certain brown sugars are made from beet and have simply been appropriately coloured. Moreover, from a strictly chemical point of view, there is no difference between refined beet sugar and sugar produced from cane.

On the other hand, coarse cane sugar, also known as raw sugar, or soft brown sugar, contains, in addition to glucids, mineral salts (mainly calcium and iron) and protid and lipid traces. Its nutritional value is, therefore, higher than that of industrially-refined sugar. It should be preferred for this reason, but consumption of it must be very moderate under any circumstances, because it is still a rapidly-assimilated sugar.

It is recommended that honey should be substituted for sugar wherever possible. Indeed, whereas white or brown sugar contains over 98 per cent saccharose, honey contains only 6 per cent: an enzyme (sucrase) which is present in bees' stomachs does, in fact, convert almost all the saccharose into glucose and fructose (around 35 per cent for each of these categories of sugar). Moreover, honey has a more powerful sweetening effect than refined sugar. Its energy supply is more quickly usable (hence its nutritional interest for sportsmen) because of the equal mix of glucose and fructose.

Finally, honey contains calcium, potassium, sodium, vitamins (in particular vitamin C) and formic acid, which has anti-infection properties for the bronchial tubes. For all these reasons honey should always be preferred to domestic sugar. It should be recalled that this substance is not recommended, as with other types of sugars, in cases of obesity, diabetes and gluco-dependent dyslipoproteinaemia.

Pastries, sweetened desserts and other sugary foods should be avoided

These culinary preparations, which are comfort foods of no nutritional interest in the strict sense, have the cumulative drawbacks of excess sugar, refined flour and 'hidden' lipids. Indeed, they are prepared with flour, sugar (sometimes replaced by honey, but that does not change very much biochemically) and butter and/or cream. We thus obtain a veritable miniature bomb which is particularly dangerous for the arteries! And the consumer believes that because of the relatively modest quantities of the ingredients he can eat them without any risk ... All these preparations, including sweets and other confectionery, should be barred from a healthy diet (a monthly exception may be allowed, subject to people being very reasonable and not making the most of the opportunity to indulge excessively). They are forbidden for all hypercholesterolaemia and obesity cases.

Cocoa and chocolate are rarely desirable

All commercial chocolates are manufactured from cocoa paste, which is quite rich in cocoa butter, sugar (in variable proportions) a mixture with or without added milk, fruit or natural or synthetic flavourings. It should be remembered that chocolates are hypercalorific (over 500 calories per 100g); they are stimulants, (because they contain theo-bromine, caffeine and phenylethylamine) and thickeners.

They are foods recommended for healthy individuals who exert considerable muscular effort and for children in moderate amounts (provided that they are not suffering from cholesterolaemia or weight problems).

Conversely, chocolates are not allowed for obese people, hypercholesterolaemic people or anyone suffering from biliary problems.

PRACTICAL ADVICE

1. Always replace white refined sugar or brown sugar with honey whenever possible.

2. Monitor your sugar and honey intake very carefully in all cases involving arterial or obesity problems.

3. Eliminate pastries, sweetened desserts and other sugary foods from your normal diet.

4. Strictly limit consumption of chocolate, which is forbidden in cases of hypercholosterolaemia or obesity.

Chapter 14

What should you drink?

Beverages, whether or not they contain alcohol, form part of the general daily diet. As such they deserve as much attention as the other types of 'foods', as they also supply certain elements, some of which are beneficial to health, others sometimes are undesirable, or even harmful.

We shall now examine these briefly:

Beer: There are a number of categories, according to their alcohol content. Table beers are 2 to 2.2 proof, bock beers 3.3 to 3.9 and luxury beers 4.4 to 6, which corresponds respectively to 16g of alcohol per litre, 25 to 30g/l and 40g/l.

The nutritional value of beer appears to be valuable at first sight. Indeed, it contains a number of mineral salts and trace elements (calcium, magnesium, phosphorus, potassium, sodium, iron, copper ...), vitamins, mainly those in group B, protids (including essential amino acids and free and combined amino acids) and various organic acids (malic, pyruvic, lactic, citric, oxalic, etc.). But this attractive picture has its downside, which involves a much greater number of disadvantages. On the one hand, all beer contains carbon dioxide (over 4.5g/l). On the other, its high calorific value is mainly supplied by glucids and especially by ethyl alcohol. A litre of beer provides as many calories as 150 to 200g of bread, which is massive.

Drinking beer is, therefore, not recommended and is even proscribed for obese persons and diabetics and in all cases of alcohol-dependent dyslipidaemia. For healthy individuals one or two pints of beer per week is more or less acceptable, subject to this not being consumed at the same time as other alcoholic drinks and to account being taken of the energy supplied in the overall daily diet intake calculation.

Wine: There are so many differences between the hundreds of varieties of wine that it is impossible to enter into any detail about their respective compositions. Only a few generalities can be stated. In favour of wine, emphasis will be placed on the fact that they are high in minerals (especially magnesium, iron and calcium), trace elements (copper, zinc, manganese, fluorine, bromine, etc.) and organic acids (particularly tartaric acid).

Moreover, very recently, two Californian specialists have produced a new hypothesis on the beneficial effect of wine on the arteries because of the presence of salicylic acid (aspirin), which appears to be excellent for the prevention of cardiovascular illnesses.

These positive elements are largely counterbalanced by the dangers presented by the regular absorption of alcohol: regularly ingested in excess it can cause very serious physiological disorders, mainly affecting the liver and brain. What is more, badly produced wine or wine containing additives (which often goes together) are veritable poisons of a very real, powerful kind.

In order to find out how to drink wine without risk we shall return to the advice given by that great heart specialist, Dr C. Barnard: *'It appears that a little alcohol each day prevents the protective cells in platelets from adhering to the walls of a damaged artery, thus preventing the formation of a blood clot or a shrinkage, which would disrupt the circulation ... A small intake of alcohol, that is, a glass of wine at lunch and another at dinner, is quite healthy. But this amount should never be exceeded.'*

Apéritifs, digestives, vermouth and other distilled alcohol (whisky, vodka, gin, etc.) are all real poisons, even outside any alcoholic addiction. They should be proscribed absolutely in all cases (whether or not one is in good health or suffering from any physical problems).

Coffee and tea, which are universal drinks, are mainly known for an alkaloid which they contain, caffeine (or theine). They also contain tannin and vitamins (especially vitamin P); their mineral contents may be considered as negligible from the nutritional point of view. The caffeine content varies considerably depending on the variety of tea and coffee and preparation (roasting, drying, grinding, etc.). In general:

1. Tea has an astringent effect on the digestion, stimulating the cerebral functions, and leads to vasomotor stimulation in small amounts; in large amounts it can cause confusion and agitation, sensorial problems, a contracturing, vasodilatory action on the peripheral circulation, acceleration of cardiac rhythm with an increase in contractility.

2.   Coffee, in small amounts, stimulates the cerebral functions, reduces drowsiness and sensitivity to fatigue, increases stimulation of the striated muscles and induces vasodilation, in particular as regards the coronary muscles; in large amounts the appearance of various problems is noticeable: mental confusion, agitation, nervous trembling, sensorial problems, contraction of the striated muscles and problems with cardiac rhythm which can extend to arrhythmia.

From the foregoing it may, therefore, be concluded that the moderate consumption of tea (two or three cups) or coffee (one or two cups per day) can have favourable effects. However, these two drinks are forbidden in cases of high blood pressure or established cardiac problems. They are not recommended either for people suffering from insomnia, anxiety or nervosism.

There is an excellent substitute product: maté, or Brazil tea. This plant, a native of South America, has been drunk by Indians for thousands of years. The leaves and small branches are used in exactly the same way as for tea. They contain chemical principles which are comparable to those of caffeine, minerals (potassium, magnesium, manganese, iron), tannin, a gelatinous substance and an alkaloid, matéin. It is a stimulant for the nervous system and has none of the disadvantages of coffee or tea. Maté can be found increasingly in Europe. We can do no more than recommend that it should be drunk instead of tea and coffee.

Fruit juices sold in the shops differ according to their designation: the simple 'fruit juice' description means that it is a drink obtained by pressing fresh, ripe fruit which has not been fermented; but this juice may have a number of products added to it: sugar, ascorbic acid, sulphurous anhydride, sorbic acid, colourants, etc.

The words 'juice based on concentrates' indicate products prepared from fruit concentrates obtained through lyophilisation; they must be diluted in the proportions of one part concentrate to eight of water. They should be avoided.

The words 'pure fruit juice' indicate that the product does not contain any additives or substances, even permitted ones (this, therefore, is the type of product which should be preferred among those on the market). These fruit juices are recommended drinks because of their high vitamin content (in particular C, B1 and B2) and certain mineral salts. Account does, however, need to be taken of the calorific value shown on the packaging.

However, you are advised to squeeze your own, at home, using good, fresh fruit which has been well-washed, without adding sugar (if need be, add a little water, particularly for children or when the squeezed fruit does not produce a lot of juice). This juice needs to be prepared daily: its nutritive value falls as time goes by, until it is no longer of much interest.

Here again, the fresh product is the one which will do your arteries good.

PRACTICAL ADVICE

1. Avoid alcoholic drinks. Two glasses of good, natural wine a day may be allowed, even recommended. After this, there are serious health risks.

2. Apéritifs, digestives, spirits, etc. are forbidden.

3. Coffee and tea may be allowed (the limit is two medium-size cups a day). However, maté should be drunk in preference to these.

4. Fruit juice prepared at home is preferable by far to all commercial products. Among the latter, those with the wording 'pure fruit juice' should be selected.

Atherosclerosis

The World Health Organization (WHO), has proposed a definition of this disease: 'Atherosclerosis is consistent with a variable combination of disorders of the intima in arteries, involving a local accumulation of lipids, complex glucids, blood and its derivatives, deposits of fibrous tissue and calcium, and associated with lesions of the media.' A Frenchman, Professor Lenègre, has defined it as follows:

Atherosclerosis is a disease of the intima of the large and medium arteries, characterised by two fundamental macroscopic lesions:

- *atheromatous plaque, consisting of lipid deposits;*

- *fibrous thickening.*

The only lipid deposit with no fibrous thickening is certainly atheroma, but it is not atherosclerosis'.

To summarise, and as our knowledge stands at present, it may be stated that atherosclerosis is a chronic degenerative disease (it begins very early and reaches an advanced stage in later life), which affects the large and medium arteries; it is characterised by the formation of yellowish plaque, called atheroma, in the intima of the vessels, followed by a proliferation of elastic fibres, atrophy of the connective tissue, calcification and necrosis, with the whole of this process moving on from the intima towards the media.

Finally, the lesions may cause obstructions or ruptures of the injured vessels.

Atherogenesis, that is, the formation of atheroma, which can take place over a number of years, is fairly well-known nowadays. Escaping detection even by radiography over a long period, the initial lesion usually occurs at vessel bifurcations and at points where the wall of an artery is somewhat delicate.

It begins by an adverse change in the elastic tissue of the intima, which loses its cohesion and becomes slightly deformed; we then witness a pathological proliferation, under the endothelium, of large, connective cells (histiocites) to which the fundamental substance attaches itself.

At this stage the body is still capable of evacuating this waste by means of complex drainage which has not been properly explained. However, this mechanism may be disturbed by various factors acting concomitantly or separately. Then, in a third phase, lipids infiltrate into the lesion: spumous cells and fatty muscular cells appear. The plaque therefore begins to take the form of a hard mass of fatty tissue, which creates turbulence in the blood flow, and to which various substances which are present in the blood (in particular platelets) begin to agglutinate.

Gradually the plaque increases in volume; the vessel becomes considerably deformed and its diameter contracts in proportion. Usually the plaque calcifies and the artery becomes fibrous. It can also ulcerate: its content, which is like a fatty pulp (atheroma is derived from the Greek athera, which means pulp) then empties into the circulatory flow. At a more advanced stage a thrombus forms in the vessel aperture, a kind of clot consisting mainly of platelet and fibrin debris. This clot can cause complete obstruction of the vessel when fully developed, or break up and trigger off arterial embolisms, or again be the source of the destruction of the elastic membranes and result in arterial aneurisms, the breaking of which is extremely serious.

How does cholesterol circulate in the body?

In order to reach the innumerable cells which need it, cholesterol is obliged to use lipoproteins as a means of transport. These are complex structures which appear as drops containing numerous lipids, in particular cholesterol, enclosed beneath a protein layer whose external wall is hydrophilic.

Let us now follow the course of exogenous cholesterol. We have had a normal meal, containing a certain amount of cholesterol. Having reached the small intestine, it is absorbed by the mucous membrane. There it is incorporated into an initial variety of lipoproteins: the chylomicrons. These will provide transportation for it in the blood and lymph to the various organs. The chylomicrons are then captured mainly by the liver, but also by other tissues. An enzyme, the lipoprotein lipase, 'digests' the chylomicrons, freeing the fatty acids which they contain and which will be burnt up on the spot. A small amount of cholesterol remains in the cells of various tissues other than those of the liver. Chylomicrons, which are present in large quantities after meals, are eliminated six to eight hours later.

The greater part of the exogenous cholesterol carried by food, and which is indestructible within the body, we should recall, rejoins, in the liver, the endogenous cholesterol synthesised by this organ. There another variety of lipoproteins becomes involved: the LDLs (abbreviation for Low Density Lipoprotein, or light lipoprotein) . Consisting of a protein wall enclosing various lipids, including cholesterol, the LDLs will transport the lipids, in the blood flow, from the liver to all the cells in the body. In fact, the cell membranes comprise LDL receivers which allow these lipoproteins to attach themselves there, then to deposit their lipids inside the cells, for use.

If matters were to remain there, the situation would quickly become catastrophic. Indeed, as cholesterol is indestructible, the cells would quickly become saturated with it and the blood would be choked by enormous amounts of LDL, with all the consequences which that involves!

This is where a third variety of lipoproteins, the HDLs, (abbreviation for High Density Lipoprotein, or heavy lipoprotein), becomes involved. Called (wrongly) 'good cholesterol' or sometimes 'cleaning lipoproteins', the HDLs capture the excess cholesterol in the cells and take it, still by means of the blood flow, to the liver. After being stored for a time it will then be incorporated into endogenous cholesterol recently manufactured by the liver and into a new batch of exogenous cholesterol.

All of this is sorted: part will be sent to the cells by a new LDL train: another part, the excess, transformed into biliary salts which will be mixed with bile and, will on the one hand, be recovered in the intestinal mucus by the chylomicrons and will return to the liver and, on the other, will be finally evacuated by the faecal bolus.

This, very simply, is the cholesterol biological cycle. (In passing we should mention the VLDLs, another category of lipoproteins of very low density which contain mainly triglycerides and small amounts of cholesterol.)

In normal circumstances the system balance is provided by the physiological regulation of the ratio between LDL and HDL cholesterol: for a certain amount of LDL, which carries cholesterol from the liver to the cells, there is a corresponding fixed amount of HDL which takes the cholesterol back to the liver. If the HDL is insufficient, there is an accumulation of LDL in the blood: this is what is known as hyperlipidaemia, or hyperlipoproteinaemia, or dyslipoproteinaemia – in short, an eminently atherogenous pathological condition.

What are 'good' cholesterol levels?

It is difficult to answer this question. Indeed, cholesterol levels vary with age, sex and a number of other considerations. The best course of action is to consult your doctor. It should, nevertheless, be pointed out that a total cholesterol level of under 2.5g/l for a mature man, with an HDL level of between 0.40 and 0.80g/l, is generally considered as being normal. For a woman who has not yet been through the menopause, these figures may be a little higher. Once again, only the doctor is in a position, after carrying out an examination, to determine the hypercholesterolaemia condition. It is best for the reader not to become obsessed with a few figures which are always difficult for the non-specialist to interpret.

Excess cholesterol and heart disease

Without a shadow of doubt there is a cause and effect relationship between hypercholesterolaemia and death from heart disease (even though excess cholesterol is not the only factor in heart attacks). Proof of this has been provided by a number of scientific studies:

a) There is a hereditary illness, which fortunately is fairly rare and can be effectively treated medically, known as family hypercholesterolaemia, characterised by a reduction in the number of LDL receivers in the cell membranes or by them being maladjusted. Children struck down by this complaint see their cholesterol levels rise to 5.5g/l in the form known as heterozygotic (only one of the parents being a carrier of the abnormality), exceed 6g/l and even reach 14g/l in the homozygous form (both parents being affected). These sick young people develop atherosclerosis very early on, particularly in the homozygous form and die of myocardial infarction, sometimes before adolescence. Significant cholesterol crystal deposits are evident, not only in the arteries, but also in the tendons and skin. In the heterozygotic form the risk of death from infarction in adulthood is multiplied by ten, if adequate treatment is not followed from an early age.

b) In 1955, Dr Ancel Keys, an American epidemiologist, compared the population of Minneapolis with that of a Bantu area in South Africa. Among the first he noted an average cholesterol level of 2.5g/l and a level of only 1.47g/l among the second. Concurrently with this he discovered that the frequency of deaths from heart attacks was six times higher among his compatriots in Minneapolis than among the Bantu!

c) Even more famous research was that carried out in Framingham, New England. For over thirty years the inhabitants of this town took part in the biological research performed by a top research team which was trying to establish whether there really was a connection between excess cholesterol and myocardial infarction. Without going into the details of the fascinating results produced by this study, which was unique in its field, it will be seen that the highest coronary incidence (12) appears with high (above 2.60g/l) total cholesterol (ChT) combined with low (lower than 0.40g/l) HDL cholesterol; that the coronary risk was three times less with ChT of 2.60 and HDL of 0.60 than with ChT of 2 and HDL of 0.40 – which clearly underlines the importance of the ChT/HDL ratio.

To sum up, we need to remember that excess cholesterol must be taken essentially as a major atherogenous factor, even when it is not associated with other factors (tobacco dependency, high blood pressure, etc.). The risk is highest when a high LDL level is noted and at the same time a low HDL level, which shows a ChT/HDL ratio of above 3. However, in its most common forms, hypercholesterolaemia is almost always linked to diet. This is the area where action needs to be taken.

Types of dyslipoproteinaemia

In its concern for therapeutic efficiency the World Health Organization (WHO) suggested classifying the different types of dyslipoproteinaemia according to the type of lipoproteins concerned. It singled out six of these:

- **Type I,** or exogenous hypertriglyceridaemia: characterised by a very high triglycerides level and a normal or slightly increased total cholesterol level. This form, which is rare and linked either to a genetic cause, or secondarily to insulin-deprived diabetes or pancreatitis, is not atherogenous; it can, however, cause severe, acute pancreatitis.

- **Type IIa,** or pure, essential hypercholesterolaemia, or LDL: characterised by a sharp increase in total cholesterol, particularly the LDL part, of normal triglycerides. It is vigorously atherogenous. Family hypercholesterolaemia belongs to this type, which can also be secondary to certain complaints (hypothyroidism, nephrosis, porphyria, cholostasis).

- **Type IIb,** or mixed hyperlipidaemia: characterised by an increase in the LDL portion, that of the VLDLs (see p. 120) and also the triglycerides. This form, which is also atherogenous, is comparable to the previous one as regards causes.

- **Type III,** or mixed hyperlipidaemia: characterised by high cholesterol and triglyceride levels. It is a rare atherogenous form, often associated with a reduction in tolerance to glucose, with obesity and also hyperuricaemia.

- **Type IV,** or endogenous hypertriglyceridaemia: a common form, characterised by a rise in triglycerides and a moderate increase in cholesterol. It is atherogenous and may be a side-effect of chronic alcoholism, sugar diabetes, nephrosis or the use of certain oral contraceptives.

- **Type V,** or mixed hyperlipidaemia, associating Types I and IV: characterised by a significant increase in triglycerides and a rise in cholesterol (chylomicrons and VLDL in particular). This form, which is atherogenous, may be of genetic origin, or a side-effect of chronic alcoholism, insulin-deprived diabetes or pancreatitis.

Annexe C

The principal hypolipaemiants and hypocholesterolaemiants

A certain number of molecules have the property of lowering lipid and cholesterol levels in the blood.

The main ones are:

- Nicotinic acid, or niacin (this is vitamin PP, designated antipellagrous): this has a vasodilatory capacity and, when taken in large doses, has a hypolemiant effect by lowering the LDL and VLDL levels. Indeed, it blocks the release of fatty acids from the adipose tissues. However, nicotinic acid does not appear to have any effect on the development of the atheromatous process. This drug is prescribed for family hypercholesterolaemia and type IV hyperlipoproteinaemia and has undesirable side-effects: hepatic problems, heartburn, diarrhoea, hyperuricaemia, nausea ...

- Resins (cholestyramin) form a family of drugs which act 'mechanically' on cholesterol of exogenous (dietary) and endogenous origin carried with the biliary salts.

These substances are capable of capturing, during intestinal transit, a part of the cholesterol present in the small intestine (that provided by food and that contained in bile). As they cannot pass through the intestinal wall they are, therefore, evacuated with the sellae, finally eliminating the amount of cholesterol captured.

The plasmatic cholesterol level falls effectively and the drug is undoubtedly innocuous. It is mainly prescribed in type II hyperlipoproteinaemia, after repeated setbacks with diet alone. However, resins involve not inconsiderable side-effects.

First, ingestion of these substances, which have an insipid, sandy texture, is not always noticeable: some patients never become used to them. Next, they greatly increase the weight of the sellae, causing considerable discomfort and sometimes severe constipation. Finally, they reduce the intestinal absorption of iron, liposoluble vitamins and a number of drugs. When they are prescribed, account should be taken of these factors.

- Fibrates (clofibrates) have been known for decades. However, the way they act has still not been properly explained. Pharmacological studies show that they spectacularly lower the triglycerides level and that they react favourably in LDL and HDL hypercholesterolaemia, but less effectively.

Indeed, the effects achieved vary considerably from one pharmaceutical speciality to another and from one patient to another. They are recommended in the event of a setback with the diet alone and in the hypertriglyceridaemia associated with LDL hypercholosterolaemia.

They have side-effects which are sufficiently serious to make their use personalised: myalgia, (muscular pain caused by the increase in a muscular enzyme, creatine-phosphokinase) the risk of biliary lithiasis, weakening of the libido, interaction with anticoagulants.

- Drugs which prevent the synthesis of cholesterol by the liver have appeared in recent times. They lower lipoproteinaemia by inhibiting the manufacture of LDL cholesterol, but have only a moderate effect on the triglyceride and HDL cholesterol levels. They are used mainly in major LDL hypercholesterolaemia, with normal or slightly raised HDL and triglyceride levels, following a setback to the diet alone.

Occasionally the treatment brings together inhibitors and resins; this type of treatment requires constant medical supervision involving, specifically, a regular dosage of various enzymes and other sanguineous biological factors. The muscular and hepatic side-effects are, in fact, considerable.

To these four types of hypolipemiant drugs three other very useful substances could be added:

- Oestrogens have a hypolipemiant action on LDL cholesterol, while at the same time increasing the 'good' HDL cholesterol level. These hormonal substances are prescribed for menopausal women for whom they provide protection against heart disease.

- Aspirin has no direct effect on cholesterol in whatever form it may be. It has, however, been known for some considerable time that this marvellous drug has a remarkable arterial, coronary and cerebral protective effect. It is, therefore, recommended for individuals exposed to the risk of atherosclerosis – provided that there are no contraindications and always under medical supervision.

- Vitamin E also has a protective property against vascular illnesses. This has been established in two very recent studies published in the *New England Journal of Medicine* (May, 1993), carried out by teams of Harvard epidemiologists in Boston.

The first one covered 87,245 women, nurses, aged 35 to 59, who were monitored over an eight-year period. The researchers established that the women whose diet was highest in vitamin E had a coronary disease risk reduced by one third in relation to those whose diet was lower in vitamin E.

The second study covered 39,910 men who were all members of the medical profession. Following very detailed monitoring over four years, the researchers established a one-third reduction in the risk of infarction in the individuals who ate the most vitamin E.

On completion of these two studies the specialists produced the hypothesis whereby the antioxidant property of vitamin E prevented the incorporation of cholesterol in the arterial wall, when the atheroma is formed.

To sum up, we should remember that:

1. There are drugs which are effective against excess cholesterol but that their use (always under medical supervision) involves side-effects which are occasionally dangerous.

2. Recourse to hypolipemiants must be envisaged by the doctor only when a dietetic regimen on its own has not made it possible to achieve a significant reduction of the cholesterol level.

3. Certain substances (oestrogens) have very valuable hypolipemiant properties, with no undesirable effects, but can be administered only to a single category of people (menopausal women).

4. Other substances (aspirin, vitamin E) have protective properties on the arteries and therefore limit the atheromatous risk.